WHY SHOULD I GO TO ROTTERDAM

WHY SHOULD I GO TO ↴
ROTTERDAM

THE CITY YOU DEFINITELY NEED TO
VISIT BEFORE YOU TURN 30 (OR 130)

THIS IS WHY!

In Rotterdam, people live by the motto *niet lullen, maar poetsen*, 'no fluff, no frills' – this city keeps it real. Its raw, authentic vibe and down-to-earth locals make it a place like no other.

Rotterdam is known for its bold, cutting-edge architecture. Right in the heart of the city, you'll find landmarks such as the Markthal, Central Station, and the Depot – a 40-metre-high mirrored bowl-shaped building with trees on its roof. Because – why not? But it's not just the architecture that makes Rotterdam. Art is everywhere. Head to Museum Park for museums galore or check out contemporary art fairs like Art Rotterdam. You'll also find art right on the streets: no other city in the Netherlands has this many outdoor sculptures. And the street art is next level. Festivals like ALL CAPS turn entire neighbourhoods into open-air galleries.

Then there's the food. Eating well is big in Rotterdam, and you'll be spoilt for choice with quirky restaurants and global flavours. With people from 170 cultures calling Rotterdam home, you can feast on everything from Surinamese *roti* and Syrian kebabs to Neapolitan pizza and Korean fried chicken. Whatever you're craving, you'll find it in Rotterdam.
When the sun sets, join a pub quiz, sip craft beers at one of the city's many indie breweries, embark on a bar crawl, hit the clubs, or dance the night away to a DJ set.

Rotterdam doesn't mess about.
So, what are you waiting for? Dive in!

CONTENTS

NEIGHBOURHOODS 8
PRACTICAL INFO 12

WHEN TO TRAVEL 28
LIFE IN ROTTERDAM 38

FOOD AND DRINKS 104
GOING OUT 128

SHOPPING 140

GREEN ROTTERDAM 168
OUTSIDE OF ROTTERDAM 182

Index 188
Who made this book? 191-192

NEIGHBOURHOODS

Centrum

Rotterdam's city centre is a hub of culture, buzzing eateries, and a vibrant nightlife. Devastated in 1940, it was quickly rebuilt, creating the bold, modern skyline you see today. Explore areas like the lively Oude Westen, packed with international cuisine and quirky shops; the city's cultural hotspot Cool; and the historic maritime quarter Scheepvaartkwartier, with stately buildings and the charming Veerhaven.

Noord

Noord is a lively neighbourhood full of charm, with 19th-century houses, fun squares, and the River Rotte — the city's namesake. Creative

DELFS

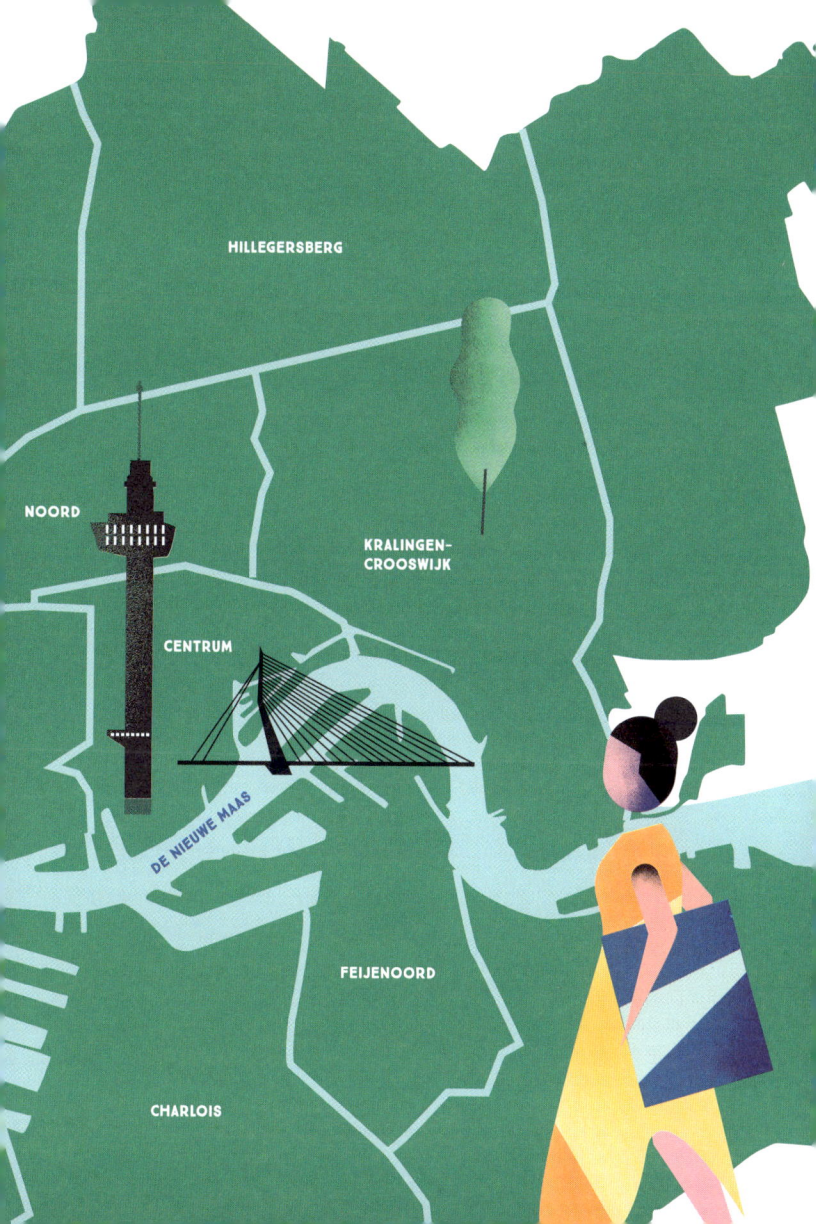

entrepreneurs have transformed it into one of Rotterdam's coolest districts, loved for boutique shopping, lovely cafés, and great dining. Nearby Blijdorp, with its iconic zoo and the laid-back Vroesenpark, adds a touch of greenery and tranquillity.

Kralingen-Crooswijk

Want to see the elegant side of Rotterdam? Kralingen is the place to be. This posh neighbourhood is known for its grand 19th-century streets and stunning villas. Wander the leafy lanes, where students and families enjoy the relaxed atmosphere. Crooswijk, on the other hand, is one of Rotterdam's most authentic neighbourhoods, packed with character and history. Once a working-class district, it has evolved into a vibrant area where old meets new. Stroll through its streets, and you'll find everything from traditional pubs to Turkish bakeries and trendy restaurants.

Feijenoord

The dynamic Feijenoord is a true melting pot, with 85 per cent of its residents having a non-Dutch background. Home to the iconic Feyenoord Stadium, it's a must-visit for football fans. But there's much more to Feijenoord than the beautiful game. Marvel at the Wilhelminapier, lined with repurposed warehouses and striking skyscrapers designed by world-famous architects, and discover creative hotspots like Katendrecht, home to museums such as the Nederlands Fotomuseum and Fenix.

Charlois

Originally a village, parts of Charlois still have this charming feel, but the district is also buzzing with new energy. It's home to Ahoy, Rotterdam's premier venue for concerts, festivals, and big events. Charlois also includes Heijplaat, nestled in the harbour. Built as a garden village for dockworkers, Heijplaat is now a hotspot for innovation and sustainability at RDM Rotterdam.

Delfshaven

In Delfshaven, you'll find a quirky mix of grand boulevards and leafy canals, and it has a vibrant multicultural energy. The old harbour is a haven for history lovers, with canals, bridges, and historic houses untouched by the city's bombing. Nearby, the M4H district is an up-and-coming hotspot. Once a bustling harbour hub, it's now Rotterdam's Makers District, buzzing with innovative start-ups, creative projects, and sustainable workshops.

Hillegersberg-Schiebroek

Rotterdam's leafy escape, where city life meets suburban charm. Known for its upscale vibe, Hillegersberg-Schiebroek offers beautiful lakes and lush parks. Whether you're sailing on the Bergse Plassen, enjoying boutique shopping, or grabbing a coffee at a fun little café, Hillegersberg-Schiebroek has a laid-back elegance.

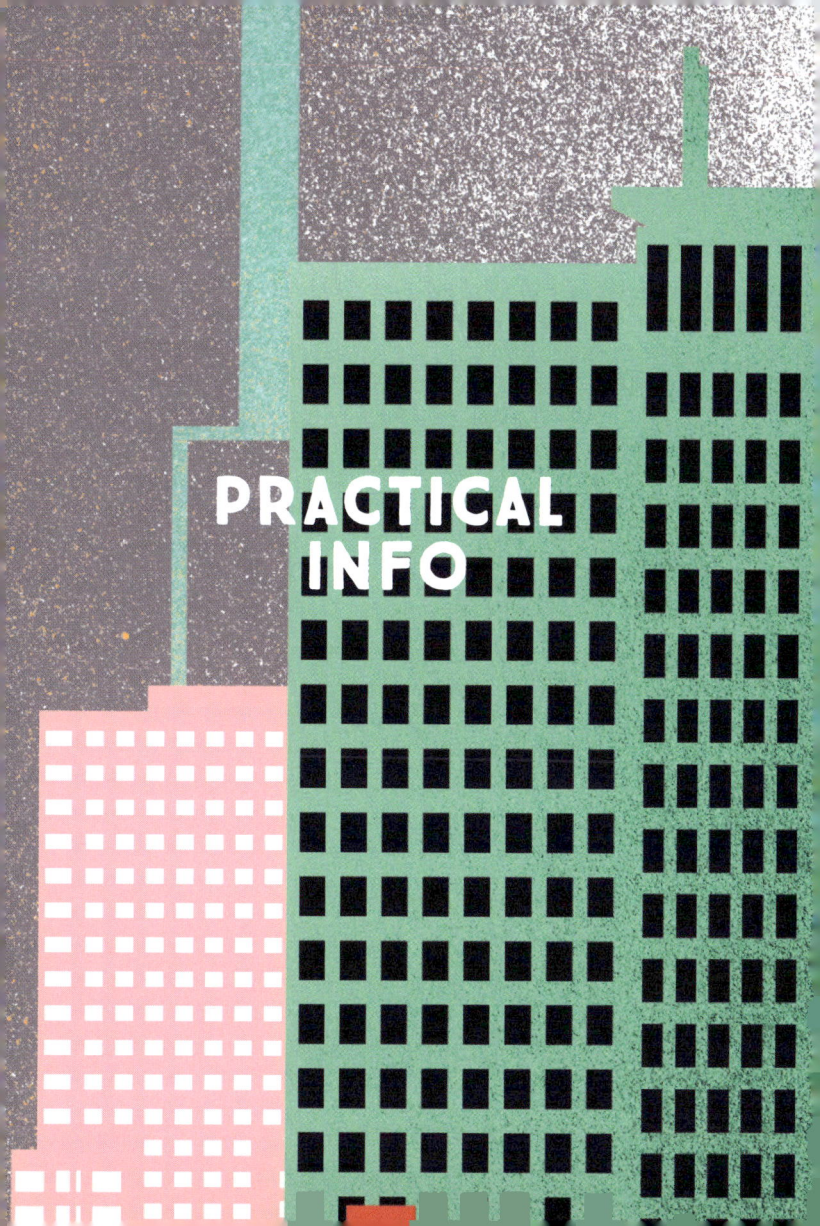

TRAVEL

Walking in Rotterdam is a fantastic way to experience the city's vibrant energy and unique mix of old and new. You can stroll along the River Maas, taking in stunning views of the iconic skyline and bold architecture. Crossing the Erasmus Bridge on foot offers both breathtaking perspectives of the city's modern marvels, as well as the historic Willemsbrug. Walking lets you discover Rotterdam's diverse neighbourhoods, hidden gems, and cultural hotspots at your own pace. From local shopping areas to little cafés and colourful street art, there's something exciting around every corner.

If walking isn't quite your thing, Rotterdam's public transport system (run by RET) makes getting around a breeze. The metro network stretches from north to south and east to west, covering almost the entire city. For areas the metro doesn't reach, such as Noord, Hillegersberg-Schiebroek or Noordereiland, trams and buses are great options. You can easily check in and out on all RET transport using your debit card, credit card, or smartphone.

Black-and-yellow boats zip across the river Maas. On request, these water taxis can take you to over fifty different stops in Rotterdam and Schiedam. Prebook your ride through the water taxi app or *watertaxirotterdam.nl*. From several spots in the city, they also run ferry services, making it a quick and convenient way to cross the river — you could fetch one from Marconistraat/M4H to go to RDM/Heijplaat, or from the city centre to Kop van Zuid. They take card payments on board. Check the water taxi website for ferry schedules.

The Netherlands is a cyclist's paradise, and Rotterdam is no exception with its dedicated bike lanes that make cycling a very convenient way to get around. Locals swear by it, and you can too. Bike-sharing systems like Lime and Donkey Republic make it easy to rent and return bikes at various locations – just download their app and you're set. Many hostels and hotels also offer bike rentals, or check out *insiderotterdam.com* who also offer guided bike tours. From April to October, you can join their city highlights tour Fridays to Sundays.

Planning to explore beyond Rotterdam? The Tourist Day Ticket is your ideal travel companion for South Holland. For just €17, this handy pass lets you hop on trams, buses, and even the Waterbus to visit cities like Delft, The Hague, and Dordrecht. You can pick one up at ticket machines on all metro stations. A ticket is valid for unlimited travel from your first check-in to the last timetabled service. Just a heads-up: this ticket doesn't cover travel on NS railway trains.

WHERE TO STAY

Stayokay Hostel Rotterdam

Overblaak 85, 3011 MH Stadsdriehoek (Centrum), stayokay.com/nl/hostel/rotterdam

Want to add a touch of fun to your stay? Stayokay Hostel Rotterdam lets you sleep in a building that looks like it's straight out of a sci-fi movie – the famous Cube Houses. Offering a cool, modern vibe, Stayokay provides comfy rooms, both private and shared, with all the essentials, like free Wi-Fi and breakfast, included.

CityHub

Witte de Withstraat 87, 3012 BN Cool (Centrum), cityhub.com/rotterdam

CityHub Rotterdam offers the perfect blend of hostel and hotel vibes. Stay in your own private cabin or 'hub' with a comfy double bed, Wi-Fi, app-controlled lighting, and personal audio streaming. The shared luxury showers and toilets are gender-separated. Located on the lively Witte de Withstraat, you'll be surrounded by bars, restaurants, and shops.

King Kong Hostel

Witte de Withstraat 72-74, 3012 BS Cool (Centrum), kingkonghostel.com

Also located on the vibrant Witte de Withstraat, King Kong Hostel is the ultimate hangout for social travellers. Meet new people at the on-site bar, grab a pizza from the menu, or treat yourself to delicious cakes from Boaz, a local baker who lives just around the corner. Relax in comfy shared dorms or private rooms, all with free Wi-Fi and modern amenities.

Pods by The Usual

Westblaak 10-14, 3012 KL Cool (Centrum), theusual.com

Fancy an eco-friendly stay? Check out The Usual's pods. Each pod is designed with a lighter footprint, thanks to organic bedding, pillows filled with recycled down and mattresses designed for circularity. Don't feel like heading out just yet? Hang out at the U Bar, where you can enjoy standout dishes like their vegan hot dog, tangy hoisin noodles, or savoury pumpkin curry.

Sparks Hostel

Westersingel 1A, 3014 GM Cool (Centrum), sparkshostel.com

The first hostel you'll find when you exit Central Station is Sparks. The hostel has a relaxed vibe and offers stylish, spacious dorms and private rooms. They all feature comfy beds, large lockers, free linen, towels, and Wi-Fi. The guest kitchen is open 24/7, equipped with everything you need to cook a tasty meal. But, with foodie paradise West-Kruiskade just around the corner, why bother?

Hostel Ani & Haakien

Coolsestraat 47-49, 3014 LC Oude Westen (Centrum), anihaakien.nl

Close to Central Station, Ani & Haakien is a quirky, creative hostel with a homely vibe. It offers comfy dorms, shared toilets and showers, a leafy garden, and a friendly communal living room to meet fellow explorers. Known for its artistic touches and local charm, the hostel is also home to Suzy the cat.

Hostel ROOM

Van Vollenhovenstraat 62, 3016 BK (Centrum), roomrotterdam.nl

Located near the picturesque Veerhaven, Hostel ROOM offers a warm, welcoming vibe with a strong community feel. There's a vibrant bar with excellent pizzas, local beers, and often live music. The hostel features 18 unique, Dutch-themed rooms – both private and shared. Start your day with a Dutch-style breakfast, which includes chocolate sprinkle sandwiches!

Motel One Rotterdam

Grotekerkplein 70, 3011 GE Stadsdriehoek (Centrum), motel-one.com/en/hotels/rotterdam/hotel-rotterdam

Affordable, modern, and perfectly located, Motel One Rotterdam is an ideal home base for your city adventures. Rooms are sleek yet practical, featuring plush beds, rain showers, and free Wi-Fi. The fun lounge doubles as a bar, offering snacks and drinks. Just steps from the Markthal and the lively Meent, it's hard to find a better spot to stay.

The James Rotterdam

Aert van Nesstraat 25, 3012 CA Cool (Centrum), thejames.nl

Bang in the centre of Rotterdam, The James offers affordable luxury with boutique charm. Stylish rooms feature comfy beds, rain showers, and free Wi-Fi. Their 24/7 Food Market offers snacks and drinks, while excellent shops, nightlife, and culture are right outside.

Hotel Not Hotel

Schaatsbaan 83, 3013 AR Oude Westen (Centrum), hotelnothotelrotterdam.com

This hotel is as unique as its name. Located close to Central Station, the creative Hotel Not Hotel is an experience in itself. Each room is designed by a local artist and hidden behind quirky façades like a giant cuckoo clock or secret bookcase. No matter which room you choose, expect bold design, comfy beds, and a cool bar serving craft cocktails and Thai bites.

↓ MOTEL ONE ROTTERDAM

The Social Hub

Willem Ruyslaan 225,
3063 ER Struisenburg
(Kralingen-Crooswijk),
thesocialhub.co/rotterdam

With its sleek rooms, co-working spaces, and vibrant communal areas, The Social Hub is perfect for both chilling out and getting stuff done. The on-site café and bar serve up great food and drinks.

Man met Bril
Koffie Hotel

Linker Rottekade 12, 3034
NT Oude Noorden (Noord),
manmetbrilkoffie.com

The rooms at Man met Bril are compact but well-designed and the vibe is extremely relaxed. The location, along the River Rotte, couldn't be any better. Man met Bril has already established quite a name in the coffee scene, so you know the coffee they serve at breakfast makes you want to jump out of bed in the morning.

PRACTICAL INFO

GOOD TO KNOW

Language

In Rotterdam, you'll have no trouble getting by in English – practically everyone speaks it, or at least thinks they do. From baristas to bus drivers, most locals are more than happy to chat in English, often with a charmingly thick Dutch accent. This delightful blend of Dutch and English, affectionately known as 'Dunglish', can lead to some hilarious phrases. Don't be surprised if someone tells you they are 'standing in the file' (stuck in traffic) or that 'bicycles hear here not' (bicycles don't belong here). Dutch kids start learning English at school from a young age, and by the time they're teenagers, they're fluent enough to binge-watch Netflix without subtitles. That's great news for visitors, because let's be honest – Dutch is notoriously tricky for foreigners. Those guttural sounds and tongue-twisting words are no joke. But if you make the effort to learn a few basics – *hallo* (hello), *dank je wel* (thank you), and the ever-useful *mag ik een biertje?* (could I have a beer?) – the locals will appreciate it. Even if they immediately switch back to English to save you the trouble.

Money

When it comes to money in Rotterdam, plastic is king. Cards are widely accepted, even in smaller shops and cafés. In fact, more and more places are moving towards a card-only policy, so don't be surprised if you find yourself unable to pay with cash at certain businesses. Contactless payments are the norm, making quick transactions a breeze. If you do need cash, euros (€) are the currency, and the best places to withdraw them are at the yellow *Geldmaat* cash points, which are widely available, or at GWK Travelex. However, if you opt for Travelex, keep an eye on the surcharge – they've been creeping up in recent years. You'll be shown the fee before completing your withdrawal, so make sure it's worth it before confirming. And if you're coming from a non-Eurozone country, be aware that dynamic currency conversion (where you're asked if you want to be charged in your local currency rather than euros) almost always results in a poorer exchange rate, so stick to euros for a better deal.

Student discount

If you're a student, good news – Rotterdam's got your back when it comes to budget-friendly options. Many museums offer discounted entry, and several cinemas – including spots like KINO, Cinerama, and LantarenVenster – knock a few euros off ticket prices for students too. Just remember to bring your student ID.

Thinking of hitting up multiple museums and attractions? Then the Rotterdam City Card might be worth looking into. It gives you at least 25% off a range of top sights, from the iconic Euromast tower to the ultra-modern Nieuwe Instituut. You can buy a card for one, two, or three days – with or without unlimited public transport – depending on how much exploring you're planning to do. Grab yours at *citycard.rotterdam. info*.

Shopping hours

In Rotterdam, shopping hours are refreshingly convenient – especially in the city centre. Most large shops are open seven days a week, typically from 10am to 7pm on weekdays and Saturdays.

Friday is *koopavond* (late-night shopping), when many shops stay open until 9pm. Some smaller, independent businesses keep to more traditional hours and may be closed on Mondays, Tuesdays, and Sundays, so it's worth checking ahead.

The Markthal, one of Rotterdam's most iconic foodie spots, is open almost daily until 8pm, with extended hours until 9pm on Fridays and slightly shorter hours on Sundays (until 6pm).

You can even shop on public holidays such as Easter, King's Day, Ascension Day (*Hemelvaartsdag*) and Pentecost (*Pinksteren*) — Rotterdam's city centre doesn't rest. The only days when most shops shut their doors are Christmas Day and New Year's Day.

As for museums, most are closed on Mondays, so plan your cultural fix for the rest of the week.

Eating habits

Rotterdam is a true metropolis, and you can find a new flavour on every corner. Thanks to the city's rich mix of cultures and nationalities, the food scene is wonderfully diverse — whether you're craving Indonesian, Surinamese, Turkish, Moroccan, Italian, Vietnamese, or anything in between, you'll find it in Rotterdam.

From trendy street food stalls to stylish restaurants and cosy neighbourhood cafés, there's something for every taste and budget. Rotterdam locals are adventurous eaters, so don't be surprised to see fusion flavours and creative twists on traditional dishes.

Coffee and brunch lovers are in for a treat too. The city is full of little cafés and hip breakfast spots where you can kick back with a flat white, tuck into a stack of pancakes, some perfectly poached eggs, or a colourful breakfast bowl that's almost too pretty to eat. A Dutch lunch tends to be fairly light — think sandwiches or a salad — and dinner traditionally starts early, often around 6pm or 7pm. But many Rotterdam restaurants work in shifts, so you'll usually have the choice to eat earlier or book a later table, whatever suits you best. Whether you're after a quick bite or a proper sit-down meal, there's no shortage of options to explore.

Paying at restaurants

The Dutch are famously thrifty (some might say a bit cheap), and no one expects generous tips. In casual restaurants, cafés or bars, rounding up to the nearest euro or leaving an extra 5-10 per cent is perfectly acceptable. In more upmarket places, a 10 per cent tip is generous but appreciated — not necessarily expected. No one's going to chase you down the street for not tipping but showing a bit of appreciation for friendly service with a couple of euros is always a nice gesture.

Bikes rule the road

Rotterdam is very bike-friendly, and cyclists *always* seem to have the right of way — at least in their minds! Keep an eye out when crossing the road, especially on the red bike paths. Don't walk on them and most definitely do not stop in the middle of one to take photos — unless you're after some angry bell ringing.

Tap water

No need to buy bottled water. Rotterdam's tap water is clean, safe, and delicious. Most restaurants are happy to give you a glass of tap water if you ask (though sometimes only if you're ordering something else).

ROTTERDAM IN SPRING

When spring hits Rotterdam, the city truly comes alive and locals flock outside to soak up the sun. Iconic outdoor hotspots reopen, like Keilecafé, Biergarten, and Garden of BIRD. For riverside fun, head to Maaskantine or Bar Stroom for drinks and a bite. For something cosier, check out De Kerktuin or Machinist aan de Cool.

Spring also means the festival season kicks off. The Rotterdam Marathon brings a city-wide buzz, with cheering crowds lining the streets. As one of the fastest marathons in the world, it attracts elite runners aiming for record-breaking times, but it's just as exciting for casual participants and spectators. On King's Day (27th April), the city turns orange for the birthday of the Dutch king. If you're in for a party, visit Kroonjuweel or Oranjebitter, or the massive Kralingse Bos Festival, where music, food, and good vibes reign supreme.

On Bevrijdingsdag (5th May), the Dutch celebrate the freedom their country has enjoyed since the end of World War II. At the free Bevrijdingsfestival in Het Park, you'll find live music, theatre performances, art installations, and delicious food. Festivals galore continue throughout spring. Dance to beats at Toffler or Vrije Volk, explore Rotterdam's rooftops during Dakendagen, or discover smaller, eclectic events scattered throughout the city. Whether you're into music, food, or culture, there's always something happening to suit your vibe.

ROTTERDAM IN SUMMER

In summer, Rotterdam transforms into an outdoor paradise. Pavement cafés fill up, parks are filled with the smokey scent of barbecues, and locals take full advantage of the warm weather. You can even swim in the city's outdoor waters, with spots like Rijnhaven, the River Rotte, and Eiland van Brienenoord offering the perfect places to cool off.

Fancy a beach day? Hop on the metro to Hoek van Holland and enjoy the sandy shores just a short ride away. After your swim, drop by Pele's Surf Shack, a relaxed beach spot serving up delicious plant-based pancakes and burgers.

When the sun sets, the fun doesn't stop. Rotterdam's nightlife spills out onto the streets, with Witte de Withstraat even closing to traffic, transforming into a pedestrian hangout. Enjoy late-night drinks at one of the many bars, soaking up the energy that pluses through the city well into the early hours.

Summer in Rotterdam also brings an explosion of festivals. Head to North Sea Jazz for world-class music, check out Keti Koti to celebrate history and heritage, or join Zomercarnaval for colourful parades and infectious beats. Inspired by the Caribbean carnival tradition, it takes over the city with dazzling costumes, energetic dance troupes, and a massive street parade. The festivities peak with the Battle of the Drums, where drum and brass bands compete in a high-energy musical showdown, making it one of the most electrifying events of the summer.

ROTTERDAM IN AUTUMN

Autumn in Rotterdam is the perfect time to embrace the crisp air and golden hues of the season. Yes, it may rain, but the city's parks transform into stunning natural backdrops, perfect for a stroll or cycle. Head to Heemraadssingel, Het Lage Bergse Bos, or Buitenplaats De Tempel to enjoy breathtaking autumn colours and warm up afterwards with a hot chocolate or a *Bock* beer in a warm café.

Autumn evenings have their own allure, especially during Grote Schijn at Kralingse Bos. This enchanting light show turns the woods into a dream-like setting, with illuminated pathways and stunning visual art that feels like stepping into a fairytale.

Rotterdam keeps the festival vibe going this time of year, with something for everyone. The Architecture Film Festival is a must for design enthusiasts, offering films about urban spaces and architecture. Music lovers shouldn't miss Left of the Dial, a multi-venue festival featuring up-and-coming alternative bands from around the world.

And if the weather's looking truly grim, Rotterdam's museums and galleries have you covered. Depot Boijmans Van Beuningen is a must-see; not just for its futuristic mirrored exterior but also for its behind-the-scenes look at how art is stored and preserved. For street art and contemporary culture, Kunsthal always has bold, rotating exhibitions that keep things fresh. Want something more offbeat? WORM is a hub for experimental art, music, and film, perfect for those who like things a little unconventional.

ROTTERDAM IN WINTER

Winter in Rotterdam brings a festive charm to the city, with Christmas markets popping up across town. At the Maker's Market in the Industriegebouw, you can find unique, handmade gifts and tasty seasonal treats. Don't miss the festive edition of Rotterdamse Oogstmarkt at Noordplein, or the magical Christmas market in Trompenburg Tuinen and Arboretum. The traditional Christmas tree in front of City Hall adds an extra sparkle to the city's winter vibe.

New Year's Eve in Rotterdam is unforgettable, with the iconic Nationaal Vuurwerk lighting up the sky above the Erasmusbrug. It's one of the biggest New Year's Eve celebrations in the Netherlands, offering a dazzling fireworks display to ring in the new year.

At the end of January, Rotterdam hosts the International Film Festival Rotterdam (IFFR), one of the city's most exciting cultural events. With screenings across the city, the festival showcases a diverse range of films from all over the world. It's the perfect opportunity to discover fresh talent, watch thought-provoking films, and party at the vibrant events happening throughout Rotterdam.

For art lovers, Rotterdam Art Week in March is a highlight, featuring Art Rotterdam, the leading con temporary art fair showcasing emerging and established artists, and OBJECT Rotterdam, a design fair where cutting-edge furniture and fashion blur the line between art and design.

HISTORY

Origins of Rotterdam

Rotterdam's origins date back to 150 CE when the area was a vast swamp traversed by the River Rotte. Small farms lined its banks, and over time, marshes were drained to create fertile farmland. From around 1200 CE, large-scale dike construction took place across the area, with the dam in the Rotte, built in 1270, which marked a key milestone. Located where you can now find the bustling Saturday market, this dam marked the birth of Rotterdam. The tiny village grew rapidly, with the first houses being built on the street we still know as Hoogstraat. By 1340, Rotterdam was granted city rights, setting it on the path to becoming the dynamic city we know today.

The Pilgrim Fathers

Did you know that a church in Rotterdam's Delfshaven has a unique connection to the Thanksgiving tradition celebrated in the U.S.A.? In 1620, a group of English religious refugees known as the Pilgrim Fathers departed from Delfshaven on the ship Speedwell, in search of a new life in the 'New World'. After the Speedwell proved unseaworthy, they joined others aboard the Mayflower in Southampton, embarking on a perilous journey to Cape Cod, Massachusetts. The Pilgrim Fathers are considered among the founders of modern America. Their 1621 harvest celebration, held to mark their first successful crop in the New World, inspired Thanksgiving, a holiday now deeply rooted in American culture, tracing its origins back to this historic journey from Delfshaven.

The 17th century

In the 17th century, Rotterdam was a city on the rise. With new harbours like Leuvehaven dug out and expanded, trade opportunities flourished. A pivotal moment came when Johan van Oldenbarnevelt, Rotterdam's city pensionary, secured a local office for the Dutch East India Company (VOC). This allowed Rotterdam to profit from the lucrative spice trade, boosting its wealth and population, and cementing its status as a major city. However, this prosperity came at a cost. Much of the success was tied to the forced labour of enslaved people, whose suffering and contributions were often overlooked. In 2021, Ahmed Aboutaleb, Rotterdam's mayor at the time, formally apologised for the city's role in the transatlantic slave trade.

Expansion of the harbour

The expansion of Rotterdam's harbour in the 18th and 19th centuries transformed the city into one of the world's largest and most important ports. By the late 19th century, increasing trade demands made it clear that Rotterdam's existing harbour facilities were insufficient. To accommodate larger ships and improve access to the North Sea, the Nieuwe Waterweg was constructed in 1872. This vital canal, designed by civil engineer Pieter Caland, established a direct and navigable route from the city to the sea, allowing Rotterdam to grow into a major international shipping hub. In the early 20th century, further harbour expansions included the development of the Merwe-Vierhavens (M4H), which became key for handling bulk goods and storing refrigerated cargo such as fruits. These new harbours positioned Rotterdam as a critical hub for agri-

cultural and industrial exports. Post-World War II, the rapid growth of global trade and industrialisation spurred the construction of the Botlek area in the 1950s. Specifically designed for chemical and petroleum industries, Botlek offered deep-water access to large tankers and extensive storage facilities, solidifying Rotterdam's reputation as the 'Gateway to Europe'.

Het Witte Huis

When Het Witte Huis ('The White House') was completed in 1898, it made history as the tallest office building in Europe. Standing 43 metres tall with eleven floors, it was a groundbreaking achievement for its time, symbolising Rotterdam's ambition and modernity. Designed by architect Willem Molenbroek, it was inspired by New York's skyscrapers. Critics were sceptical, calling the project overly ambitious and even dangerous, but Het Witte Huis proved them wrong. Its elegant white façade, adorned with Art Nouveau details, quickly became a landmark. The building's success set a new standard for modern construction in Europe. Remarkably, Het Witte Huis survived the heavy bombing of Rotterdam during World War II, making it one of few historic buildings still standing in the city today.

The bombing

On 14th May 1940, Rotterdam experienced one of the most devastating events in its history. As part of Germany's invasion of the Netherlands, the Luftwaffe carried out a massive aerial bombardment of the city's centre. Within minutes, the heart of Rotterdam was engulfed in flames, and nearly 25,000 homes and countless cultural landmarks were destroyed. Over 800 people lost their lives. The attack aimed to pressure the

Dutch government into surrendering, and it succeeded; the Netherlands capitulated the following day. The bombing ignited fires that raged for several days, with firefighters and emergency services working tirelessly to control the flames. It took approximately three days to extinguish the inferno, but by then, much of Rotterdam's city centre lay in ruins, its landscape forever altered by the devastation.

The reconstruction

The city wasted no time in planning its reconstruction. Just a day after the devastation, city leaders, including the mayor, councillors, and architects, gathered to discuss the rebuild. Rather than simply restore what had been lost, Rotterdam decided to embrace innovation and modernity. In 1946, the city adopted a Basic Plan that set the direction for its future. The plan called for wide streets, open spaces, and bold new architectural styles that would replace the narrow alleys and traditional buildings of the past. One of the standout features of this new Rotterdam was the creation of Lijnbaan, Europe's first car-free shopping street, which became an iconic symbol of the city's modernisation. Another significant change was the focus on collective buildings. The Basic Plan encouraged modern, functional architecture, freeing it from earlier urban planning restrictions. This led to the creation of iconic buildings like Groot Handelsgebouw and Industriegebouw, developed in the 1950s, which became symbols of Rotterdam's post-war architectural transformation.

Modern architecture

Rotterdam's bold approach to rebuilding helped shape a new architectural identity. Its forward-thinking attitude continued throughout the 20th century, with architects con-

stantly experimenting with new styles and materials. As a result, Rotterdam became known for its striking, modern skyline, with buildings that stand out for their creativity as well as practicality. Today, the city is home to some of the world's most impressive examples of contemporary architecture, like the Cube Houses, Markthal, and Depot Boijmans van Beuningen. Rotterdam's focus on innovation and its ability to embrace change made it a leader in modern architecture.

The European Cup

In May 1970, Rotterdam was buzzing with excitement as Feyenoord made history winning the European Cup. A first for a Dutch football club. On 6th May, Feyenoord faced Celtic in the final at the San Siro in Milan and came out victorious with a 2-1 win. The following day, the team returned to Rotterdam with the trophy. Over 100,000 ecstatic fans gathered in the city centre to celebrate, with the team appearing on the balcony of City Hall. The European Cup was displayed in a pavilion on Coolsingel, allowing fans to pose alongside it. People queued for six hours, waiting for their turn. This unforgettable event, known as *Met de Cup op de Kiek* (Snap a Pic with the Cup), became a symbol of Rotterdam's football pride and is still remembered as a historic moment in the city's sporting history.

IFFR

The International Film Festival Rotterdam (IFFR) has been a key cultural event in the city since 1971. Over the years, it has grown into one of Europe's largest film festivals, celebrated for showcasing innovative and independent films. The festival has introduced groundbreaking works and directors to the world, including early films by renowned directors like Martin Scorsese and Lars von Trier. The Tiger

Award, introduced in 1995, has become a prestigious recognition for emerging talent. IFFR's commitment to diversity, sustainability, and its international reach have made it a favourite among film lovers. Today, the festival attracts thousands of visitors annually, continuing to be a major highlight of Rotterdam's cultural calendar.

Hardcore vibes

In the 1990s, hardcore music became the defining sound of Rotterdam, sparking a cultural movement that resonated with young people across the city and eventually the country. DJs like Rob from Parkzicht, Paul Elstak, Charlie Lownoise, and Mental Theo were at the forefront, creating high-energy tracks that defined the era. Rotterdam Terror Corps amplified the scene with their intense performances, becoming iconic figures in the hardcore world. The Energiehal, known as the '*gabber* temple of Europe', was at the epicentre of this movement. Thousands of fans flocked to its legendary parties, losing themselves in the beats and euphoric atmosphere. Hardcore went beyond the music — it was a way of life. A combination of Aussie tracksuits, Air Max trainers, and small sunglasses created a signature look. And hardcore in Rotterdam wasn't just a genre; it was a rebellious and expressive subculture that united a generation and cemented the city's reputation as a global hub for hardcore music.

SIGHTSEEING

Erasmusbrug

Erasmusbrug 1, 3011 BN Scheepvaartkwartier (Centrum)

This stunning bridge connects Rotterdam's city centre with the southern district. Designed by Ben van Berkel, the Erasmusbrug has been a defining feature of the city since 1996 and is affectionately called 'The Swan' by locals due to its graceful design. Whether you're walking, cycling, driving, or taking the tram, the bridge offers a perfect route to explore both sides of the city. For the best views, head to the water or Noordereiland, where you can fully appreciate the beauty of this iconic structure.

Laurenskerk

Grotekerkplein 15, 3011 GC Stadsdriehoek (Centrum), laurenskerkrotterdam.nl

Standing tall at 65 metres, the Laurenskerk may not be the tallest building in Rotterdam, but it's one of the city's few remaining medieval structures. This historic church, heavily damaged in the 1940 bombing, was beautifully restored and now stands as a powerful symbol of resilience. Its impressive wooden ceiling and grand interior make it a must-visit. From April to October, you can go on a guided tower climb for stunning views over the city. Just outside, on Grotekerkplein, the bronze statue of Erasmus is said to turn a page of his book every time the church clock strikes the hour.

Markthal

Ds. Jan Scharpstraat 298, 3011 GZ Stadsdriehoek (Centrum), markthal.nl

A foodie's paradise and an architectural wonder in one: that is Markthal. Designed by MVRDV architects, this striking horseshoe-shaped building is home to one hundred market stalls offering everything from fresh produce to international delicacies. Its modern design is inspired by Southern European markets but with a bold, contemporary twist. Look up, and you'll see the breathtaking artwork *Hoorn des Overvloeds* ('Horn of Plenty'), a massive 11,000-square-metre ceiling masterpiece by artists Arno Coenen and Iris Roskam. Just outside, on Binnenrotteplein, Rotterdam's traditional open-air market takes place every Tuesday and Saturday, adding to the lively atmosphere.

Oude Haven

Oudehavenkade, 3011 MG Stadsdriehoek (Centrum), oudehaven.nl

The Oude Haven ('Old Harbour') is one of Rotterdam's most vibrant spots, where history meets a buzzing nightlife. It was created after the dam was built in the River Rotte, marking the city's very beginnings. Today, the harbour is home to historic ships that gently bob in the water, creating a unique contrast with the modern skyline. Cosy cafés, bars, and lively outdoor seating areas line the waterfront, attracting many young people and students looking for a great night out. The striking Witte Huis only adds to the charm.

Kubuswoningen

*Overblaak, 3011 MH
Stadsdriehoek (Centrum)*

One of Rotterdam's most striking architectural wonders is a collection of bright yellow, tilted cubes that seem to defy gravity. Designed in the 1980s by architect Piet Blom, these Cube Houses (*Kubuswoningen*) were created to form a small village within the city. Also known as *Blaakse Bos* ('Blaak Forest'), the houses are tilted at a 45-degree angle, making them look like a futuristic puzzle. Even more surprising is that people actually live in them! Their unique design turns a simple walk through the area into a fascinating experience. Curious to see inside? One Cube, known as *Kijk-Kubus*, is open to visitors.

Veerhaven

Veerkade, 3016 DE Scheepvaartkwartier (Centrum), veerhavenrotterdam.nl

This charming harbour is tucked away in the heart of Rotterdam, offering a glimpse into the city's maritime history. With its rows of classic 19th-century buildings and docked boats, it feels like stepping back in time. The area has a relaxed vibe, perfect for a stroll or a drink by the water at one of the vibrant cafés. Veerhaven attracts both locals and visitors, making it an ideal spot to unwind and enjoy the view. It's a hidden gem in the city, combining history, beauty, and a laid-back atmosphere all in one.

Euromast

*Parkhaven 20, 3016 GM
Scheepvaartkwartier (Centrum), euromast.nl*

Built for the 1960 Floriade, this towering structure stands as a symbol of Rotterdam's innovation and ambition. Originally a temporary feature for the horticultural exhibition, it quickly became a permanent part of the skyline thanks to its stunning views of the city and beyond. At 185 meters tall, it offers one of the best vantage points in Rotterdam, where you can catch breathtaking sights of the harbour, Erasmusbrug, and the city's dynamic architecture. But it's not just a lookout point — inside, you'll find a restaurant and even a hotel room suspended in the sky! For an extra thrill, you can take a ride in the glass elevator or try abseiling down the side.

Delfshaven

Voorhaven 16, 3024 RM Delfshaven-Schiemond (Delfshaven), historischdelfshaven.nl

If you're looking for a break from Rotterdam's modern skyline, head to charming Delfshaven. This historic part of the city survived both the bombing and the urban renewal, offering a glimpse into Rotterdam's past. Originally part of Delft, Delfshaven was annexed by Rotterdam in 1886. You'll find picturesque historic canals and quaint canal houses that give the area a unique atmosphere. Key landmarks include the Pilgrim Fathers Church, the local brewery De Pelgrim, and the iconic windmill, Korenmolen De Distilleerketel. Delfshaven also boasts galleries, cosy cafés, and quirky antique shops, making it a perfect spot for a leisurely stroll through Rotterdam's past.

Floating Farm

Gustoweg 10, 3029 AS Nieuw Mathenesse (Delfshaven), floatingfarm.nl

Rotterdam's Floating Farm is the first of its kind, bringing farming back to the city in a whole new way. The idea is to raise awareness about sustainable farming by using circular practices that reduce transport emissions and waste. On your visit, you can learn all about the cows and their

Van Nellefabriek

Van Nelleweg 1, 3044 BC Spangen (Delfshaven), vannellefabriekrotterdam. com

unique floating home and even pick up some fresh dairy products from the shop. It's a clever, innovative example of how Rotterdam is blending modern city life with sustainability.

The Van Nellefabriek is an iconic example of Dutch modernism. Designed by Brinkman & Van der Vlugt, this massive industrial complex revolutionised architecture by giving new meaning to air, light, and space. Completed in 1930, the factory produced tobacco, coffee, and tea, becoming a hub of industrial innovation. Le Corbusier called it 'the most beautiful spectacle of modern times', and in 2014, it earned UNESCO World Heritage status. You can explore the factory during a guided tour by Chabot Museum staff on weekends (book in advance).

ss Rotterdam

3e Katendrechtse Hoofd 25, 3072 AM Katendrecht (Feijenoord), ssrotterdam.nl

Step back in time aboard the ss Rotterdam and discover the fascinating history of this iconic ship. Launched in 1959, it made its maiden voyage to New York, followed by decades of cruises around the globe. Today, the ship is docked in Katendrecht and serves as a unique hotel. The 576 original cabins have been beautifully restored, with the higher decks offering more luxurious rooms. You'll find a variety of restaurants and bars on board. For something different, you can test your skills in the escape room located in the old cold storage or take a guided tour to learn more about the ship's fascinating story.

↓ FLOATING FARM

↓ VAN NELLEFABRIEK

SIGHTSEEING

MUSEUMS & GALLERIES

Galerie Vivid

Scheepmakershaven 17, 3011 VA Stadsdriehoek (Centrum), galerievivid.com

Since 1999, this art gallery has been a go-to spot for cutting-edge art and design. It was one of the first to showcase design as art, featuring big names like Studio Job, Hella Jongerius, and Jaime Hayon. Today, Galerie Vivid continues to present groundbreaking work from both emerging and established designers. You'll find it in the Red Apple tower.

Kunstblock

Witte de Withstraat 50, 3012 BR Cool (Centrum), kunstblock.nl

Curious what makes Witte de Withstraat Rotterdam's cultural hotspot? Head to Kunstblock's weekly *Kunstavond*. Every Friday from 6 to 9pm you can enjoy free access to exciting art spaces like V2_, WORM, MaMa, and Kunstinstituut Melly, offering exhibitions, performances, and more. With a fresh, diverse programme each week, it's a vibrant way to dive into Rotterdam's arts scene.

Kunsthal

Westzeedijk 341, 3015 AA Dijkzigt (Centrum), kunsthal.nl

Big names, bold exhibitions – Kunsthal Rotterdam has it all. Unlike most museums, it has no permanent collection, so there's always something new to discover. From Ai Weiwei's thought-provoking art to Jean-Paul Gaultier's iconic fashion, its ever-changing shows span photography, design, and contemporary art. A dynamic space that keeps culture lovers coming back for more.

Natuurhistorisch Museum

Westzeedijk 345, 3015 AA Dijkzigt (Centrum), hetnatuurhistorisch.nl

Weird, wild, and wonderfully fascinating – that's Natuurhistorisch Museum. Packed with skeletons and taxidermy, its star attraction is Ramon, the famous Asian elephant from Blijdorp Zoo. Don't miss *Dead Animals with a Story*, a hilariously dark exhibit featuring legends like *Dominomus*, the sparrow that was shot for toppling 23,000 dominoes during the 2005 TV show Domino Day. Science, nature, and a dose of humour await.

Nieuwe Instituut

Museumpark 25, 3015 CB Dijkzigt (Centrum), nieuweinstituut.nl

Bold ideas and cutting-edge design come to life at Nieuwe Instituut, Rotterdam's hub for architecture, design, and digital culture. With ever-changing exhibitions, it explores everything from futuristic cities to sustainable fashion. The striking building itself is a modern masterpiece.

↓ KUNSTHAL (STATUE BY THOMAS J. PRICE)

↓ KUNSTHAL

Chabot Museum

Museumpark 11, 3015 CB Dijkzigt (Centrum), chabotmuseum.nl

Set in a beautiful white villa, Chabot Museum is all about the bold, expressive art of Dutch painter and sculptor Henk Chabot. His powerful works, including haunting WWII portraits and vibrant landscapes, take centre stage. With its light-filled spaces and modernist vibe, this small museum is a hidden gem for art lovers in Rotterdam.

Huis Sonneveld

Jongkindstraat 12, 3015 CG Dijkzigt (Centrum), nieuweinstituut.nl/projects/huis-sonneveld

Step into the 1930s at Huis Sonneveld, one of the best-preserved Modernist homes in the Netherlands. Designed by Brinkman and Van der Vlugt, this museum house shows how a prominent Rotterdam family embraced sleek design, open spaces, and cutting-edge tech of the time. A time capsule of the Nieuwe Bouwen movement, it's like walking into the future – past style.

Depot Boijmans van Beuningen

Museumpark 24, 3015 CX Dijkzigt (Centrum), boijmans.nl/depot/

Art lovers, this is your dream destination! Unlike most museums, Depot Boijmans Van Beuningen lets you see its entire collection – no hidden storage here. Watch conservators restore masterpieces and explore thousands of artworks. Designed by MVRDV, the architects behind the Markthal, its mirrored, bowl-shaped building is a spectacle on itself. Head to the rooftop for breathtaking views over Rotterdam.

Museum Rotterdam '40-'45 NU

Coolhaven 375, 3015 GC Dijkzigt (Centrum), museumrotterdam.nl

Immerse yourself in Rotterdam's darkest days at Museum Rotterdam '40 - '45 NU. This gripping experience puts you in the heart of the city during the devastating 1940 bombing, with personal stories, haunting images, and immersive soundscapes. A powerful look at WWII's impact on Rotterdam — and essential for truly understanding the city's history.

Wereldmuseum

Willemskade 25, 3016 DM Scheepvaartkwartier (Centrum), wereldmuseum.nl

Housed in a stunning 1851 building that once belonged to Prince Hendrik's Royal Yacht Club, Wereldmuseum offers a diverse collection of art and cultural treasures from around the world. Alongside its permanent exhibits, the museum hosts temporary exhibitions on a wide range of fascinating topics. It's the perfect place to explore new cultures and dive into history.

Galerie Wind

Prins Hendrikkade 124A, 3071 KL Noordereiland (Feijenoord), galeriewind.nl

Galerie Wind is a well-known name in Rotterdam's art scene, known for its inclusive approach to visual art. Founded by Ellen Wind, the gallery offers both emerging and established artists a platform to showcase their work through surprising and thought-provoking exhibitions. Although Ellen sadly passed away in 2024, the gallery continues to thrive, staying true to her vision.

Fenix

Veerlaan 21, 3072 AN Katendrecht (Feijenoord), fenix.nl

Explore migration through the eyes of artists at Fenix. It tells the stories of migrants from all over the world, with stunning views of the quay where millions once embarked on a journey, in search of a better life. The museum, housed in the renovated Fenixloods II, features a sleek, twisting Tornado staircase by MAD Architects that leads to a 360-degree rooftop vista.

Nederlands Fotomuseum

Brede Hilledijk 95, 3072 KD Katendrecht (Feijenoord), nederlandsfotomuseum.nl

Step into the world of Dutch photography at Nederlands Fotomuseum, home to iconic works by Ed van der Elsken, Cas Oorthuys, and contemporary talents like Viviane Sassen. Now housed in the historic Pakhuis Santos, the museum spans eight floors of exhibitions, studios, and a photography bookshop. Don't miss the rooftop restaurant with stunning Rotterdam skyline views.

↓ 'SYLVETTE' BY PABLO PICASSO AND CARL NESJAR

↓ DEPOT BOIJMANS VAN BEUNINGEN

Huidenclub

*Pelgrimsstraat 5C,
3029 BH, Schiemond
(Delfshaven), huiden.club*

Once a leather factory, now a buzzing creative hub — Huidenclub blends art, design, and entrepreneurship. It's a dynamic space with exhibitions, performances, talks, and screenings, plus workspaces where artists, designers, and entrepreneurs collaborate. It's a playground for bold ideas and fresh talent, perfect for anyone curious about Rotterdam's vibrant underground art scene.

Brutus

*Keileweg 10-18, 3029 BS,
Nieuw Mathenesse
(Delfshaven), brutus.nl*

Raw, edgy, and unapologetically bold — that's Brutus. Housed in an industrial space, it showcases contemporary art and experimental projects. The mastermind? Joep van Lieshout, whose work shines in Brutus Base. Explore ever-changing exhibitions in Brutus Space and wander through Brutus Garden, a free sculpture park packed with striking pieces.

↓ FENIX

STREET ART

Rotterdam as a whole is an open-air art gallery, home to more murals and public sculptures than any other Dutch city. It began in 1622 with the statue of Erasmus, and now you can spot works by big names like Rodin, Willem de Kooning, and Karel Appel. Stroll the Sculpture Route (*Beeldenroute*) along the Westersingel to spot iconic pieces or look up to see vibrant murals brightening the cityscape.

ALL CAPS

all-caps.nl

Rotterdam's annual street art festival turns entire neighbourhoods into canvases for incredible murals. International artists transform areas like Afrikaanderwijk, Feijenoord, and Beverwaard with bold, colourful works. An online map guides visitors to each mural.

Rewriters Rotterdam

rewriters010.nl

The Rewriters Rotterdam app offers self-guided street art tours across Rotterdam and takes you on a journey along vibrant murals, showcasing both local and international artists. Learn the stories behind the artworks and discover hidden gems throughout Rotterdam.

Cascade

Coolsingel, 3011 AG Cool (Centrum)

Nicknamed *'de Druiper'*, this striking sculpture by Atelier van Lieshout features stacked oil barrels, forming a towering column dripping a thick liquid, revealing human forms. The work blends hard and soft elements, symbolising power, struggle, and the city's industrial roots.

De Verwoeste Stad

Plein 1940, 3011 EA Stadsdriehoek (Centrum)

One of the most iconic war monuments in Western Europe, Ossip Zadkine's *De Verwoeste Stad* symbolises Rotterdam's devastation during WWII. The figure, known as *'Jan Gat'* or *'Jan met de Handjes'*, has arms raised in anguish and a dramatic hole in its torso, representing the city's shattered heart after the 1940 bombings. Every year, on 14th May, a memorial takes place at its foot.

Santa Clause

Eendrachtsplein, 3012 LA Cool (Centrum)

The sculpture *Santa Clause*, known locally as *'Kabouter Buttplug'*, is a provocative work by artist Paul McCarthy. With its oversized gnome figure and playful yet cheeky design, it adds a touch of humour and controversy to the streets of Rotterdam. Daring, and definitely attention-grabbing, it's a sculpture that sparks conversation.

Moments Contained

Stationsplein, 3013 AJ Cool (Centrum)

Standing tall outside Rotterdam's Central Station, *Moments Contained* by Thomas J. Price is a striking bronze sculpture of a casually dressed young woman with her hands tucked in her pockets, radiating quiet confidence. Like many sculptures in Rotterdam, it has a playful nickname: *'Knotje van Rotje'* ('Rotje's Bun'), with a nod to her signature hairstyle. A modern icon with serious-cool vibes.

Maasbeeld

Bolwerk, Stadsdriehoek (Centrum)

This sculpture was designed by Auke de Vries in 1981, inspired by the sleek lines of the new Willemsbrug. *Maasbeeld*, or *'De Waslijn'*, creates a horizontal connection from the bridge to an old pillar, featuring elements like rings and boxes from the maritime world. It interacts with its surroundings, gently moving with the wind and Maas water.

Tymon de Laat

tymondelaat.com

The work of this talented Rotterdam-based visual artist and muralist often reflects his travels through Latin America. Tymon de Laat creates vibrant portraits of people he meets during his trips. His stunning murals, like the powerful depiction of singer Jeangu Macrooy at Ahoy, the earthy *Madre Tierra* on Bergweg, and *Zodiac* on West-Kruiskade, captivate the city's streets with their striking colours and cultural depth.

West-Kruiskade

West-Kruiskade, Oude Westen (Centrum), rotterdamstreet-artmuseum.com

That same West-Kruiskade was dubbed the Rotterdam Street Art Museum in 2017. Home to murals by both local and international artists, it showcases stunning works, including those by Tymon de Laat. Just stroll along West-Kruiskade and 1e Middellandstraat, and you'll find colourful murals on almost every wall, making it an urban art haven.

Rotterdam Art Ride

Maashaven O.Z., Afrikaanderwijk (Feijenoord), foundationmesh.com/roar

For this massive outdoor art project, eighteen metro pillars between Rijnhaven and Maashaven were transformed into vibrant masterpieces. Created by a mix of emerging and established artists from all over Europe, the colourful artworks aim to inspire locals and bring more life to the neighbourhood. This creative route along the Maashaven quay connects Katendrecht and Afrikaanderwijk, bringing a unique cultural energy to the area.

CINEMA

In the Netherlands, dubbing is reserved for kids' films because Dutchies love to watch their films in the original language. Whether it's English, French, or Korean, films are screened in their original language with Dutch subtitles.

Pathé Schouwburgplein

Schouwburgplein 101, 3012 CL Cool (Centrum), pathe.nl

Right in the heart of Rotterdam, Pathé Schouwburgplein is perfect for catching the latest Hollywood hits. With its modern vibe, comfy seats, and huge screens, it's a popular spot.

Cinerama

Westblaak 18, 3012 KL Cool (Centrum), cineramabios.nl

Cinerama has been a staple of Rotterdam's film scene since the 1960s. This cosy cinema screens a mix of quality blockbusters and accessible arthouse films, attracting a diverse crowd. Its vintage façade and 1957 wall mosaic make it a charming municipal monument.

Kino

Gouvernestraat 129-133, 3014 PM Oude Westen (Centrum), kinorotterdam.nl

This is Rotterdam's go-to spot for film lovers, blending the best of new releases with cult classics and themed screenings. Set in the original LantarenVenster building, Kino's got serious style. Hungry? Niko's serves tasty burgers.

CineNoord

Bergweg 283, 3037 EM
Liskwartier (Noord),
cinenoord.nl

Every Thursday night, CineNoord brings films to life at Studio de Bakkerij. Each film is introduced by a film expert or special guest, often followed by interviews or debates that delve into current events and thought-provoking themes.

LantarenVenster

Otto Reuchlinweg
996, 3072 MD Kop
van Zuid (Feijenoord),
lantarenvenster.nl

LantarenVenster is a vibrant cultural hotspot on the Kop van Zuid. As the city's largest arthouse cinema, it screens everything from Oscar winners to classics and docs. Grab a bite with a view of the Rijnhaven at its café-restaurant.

↓ KINO

FESTIVALS

IFFR

Every January, Rotterdam transforms into a haven for film lovers with bold, independent films from around the world. From underground gems to big-screen premieres, this festival is a must-do. Expect screenings, Q&As, parties, and a buzzing creative vibe across the city's coolest cinemas.

iffr.com

MOMO

A three-day multidisciplinary festival in April that turns Rotterdam into a playground for music, art, and adventure. From big names to hidden gems, expect mind-blowing performances in unexpected locations. Discover new sounds, explore unique venues, and soak up the creative energy.

motelmozaique.nl

Toffler Festival

Rotterdam's ultimate electronic music festival, where the city's industrial vibe meets cutting-edge beats. With top DJs and immersive visuals, it transforms Roel Langerakpark into an electrifying dance floor. Expect non-stop energy, incredible soundscapes, and a crowd ready to party till dawn. One day at the end of May.

Roel Langerakweg, 3041 JK Blijdorpse polder (Noord), tofflerfestival.nl

Rotterdamse Dakendagen

During this festival, rooftops that are usually off-limits open up for epic views, live music, art, and adventure. Climb hidden spots, explore rooftop bars, and see Rotterdam from a whole new perspective – literally. Ten days in late May / early June.

rotterdamsedakendagen.nl

Keti Koti

From the end of June, reflections on slavery and the colonial past in Suriname and the former Netherlands Antilles are marked by a Remembrance Service, guest speakers, and performing arts. On 1st July, the abolition of slavery in the former Dutch colonies is commemorated with Keti Koti ('chains broken' in Sranan Tongo), and celebrated at two Rotterdam locations. The event consists of Bigi Spikri, mirroring the parade held by newly freed people in 1863, a food market, and performances by artists from the Afro-Caribbean diaspora.

Schouwburgplein, 3012 CL Cool (Centrum); Wijkpark Oude Westen 3014 PZ Oude Westen (Centrum), ketikotirotterdam.nl

Rotterdam Unlimited Zomercarnaval

For one day in July, Rotterdam pulses with Caribbean and Latin vibes. The Zomercarnaval Streetparade is a 2.5 km explosion of colour, music, and high-energy dancing. With over 2,500 dancers, 25 carnival troupes, DJs, and iconic floats, this is the largest Caribbean street party in the Netherlands, and you're invited to dance.

rotterdamunlimited.com

DÂK

Hidden above a parking garage near Witte de Withstraat, this summer pop-up festival is pure rooftop magic. Six days a week, enjoy live music, club nights, tasty food, and even a ping-pong competition. Enter through a secret alleyway and discover one of Rotterdam's coolest summer spots. Four weeks from mid-July to mid-August.

Apcoa Parking Westblaak, Hartmansstraat 35, 3012 VA Cool (Centrum), dak-rotterdam.nl

Blijdorp Festival

One of the leading music festivals, Blijdorp blends electronic beats, art, and nature into one unforgettable summer day in August. Set in a lush park, this vibrant fest brings top DJs, live acts, and creative surprises. Think dreamy stages, great vibes, and a crowd ready to dance from day to night.

Roel Langerakweg, 3041 JK Blijdorpse polder (Noord), blijdorpfestival.nl

Roffa Mon Amour

For twelve days in August, this quirky open-air film festival celebrates global cinematic talent, showcasing films at night in a playful venue. It's the perfect place to discover unexpected gems, with thought-provoking screenings, creative vibes, and a community of film lovers coming together.

roffamonamour.com

Left of the Dial

Discover the best new international bands at this cutting-edge music festival. From indie to metal, alt-folk to dance punk, and everything in between — Left of the Dial is all about the fresh sounds. With gigs across 22 venues, it's a citywide celebration of next-gen music. Three days in October.

leftofthedial.nl

THINGS TO DO

RiF010

Ever heard of an urban surf pool? At RiF010, a special wave-making installation creates the perfect environment. Beginner or pro, you can catch some great waves. You can also take diving lessons, rent kayaks or SUPs, or just chill at the beach-style bar.

Steiger 2, 3011 GT Stadsdriehoek (Centrum), rif010.nl

HotTug

If you fancy a chilled experience on the water, hop into a HotTug, a wood-fired floating hot tub. Sail along Rotterdam's canals while staying warm and relaxed, taking in the city's views. You can even pour yourself a cocktail on board. Visit gastropub V11 to explore rental options.

Wijnhaven 101, 3011 WN Stadsdriehoek (Centrum), hottug.nl

DakAkker

Looking for a surprising green space? Head to Schiekade 189, take the lift to the top, and climb up to DakAkker, a rooftop urban farm offering stunning views of Rotterdam's city centre. Herbs, veggies, and edible flowers are grown here, which are freshly picked and served at nearby restaurants. A hidden gem for nature lovers.

Schiekade 189, 3013 BR CS-kwartier (Centrum), dakakker.nl

Brouwerij Noordt

Visit Brouwerij Noordt, a local brewery in a former fire station by the River Rotte. They craft beers like IPA, *tripels*, and refreshing white ales. Better taste them at their taproom while the brewing process happens right beside you.

Join a tour on a Friday or Saturday afternoon, with two beers included in the price.

Zaagmolenkade 46, 3035 KA Oude Noorden (Noord), brouwerijnoordt.nl

Harbour dip

On a hot day, take a refreshing dip in the Rijnhaven. At the floating park near LantarenVenster, there's a designated safe area to relax or take a dip. Dive in, make a splash off the quay, and enjoy stunning views of Rotterdam's sleek, modern architecture while you swim.

Antoine Platekade 997, 3072 ME Kop van Zuid (Feijenoord)

Excursion M4H

Join an UrbanGuides walking tour through Rotterdam's dynamic M4H area, where old warehouses and industrial heritage meet new creative ventures. Discover the rich history, iconic spots like the HAKA building and Citrusveiling, and innovative projects such as the Floating Farm and Keilepand. A perfect mix of past, present, and future.

urbanguides.nl

FAMOUS PEOPLE

Bep van Klaveren

A true Rotterdam fighter, Bep van Klaveren became a national hero by winning Olympic gold in boxing at the 1928 Amsterdam Games. Known as 'The Dutch Windmill' for his relentless style, he put Rotterdam on the boxing map. Having grown up in a tough working-class neighbourhood, he embodied the city's no-nonsense, never-give-up attitude. Even after his career, his legacy lived on, inspiring generations of boxers and earning him a statue in his beloved hometown.

Davina Michelle

Davina Michelle took the Dutch music scene by storm with her powerful vocals. She rose to fame by posting cover songs on YouTube, with her rendition of *What About Us* catching the attention of Pink, who praised it as 'better than I will ever sound'. Since then, Davina's career has skyrocketed, including playing support for big artists like Robbie Williams. Known for her unique sound and stage presence, the Rotterdam singer continues to make waves globally.

Erasmus

Desiderius Erasmus was a philosopher, humanist, and scholar who shaped the Renaissance with his ideas on education, religion, and free thought. Through his vast number of translations, books, essays, prayers, and letters, he is considered one of Europe's most influential thinkers. Born in Rotterdam in the late 1460s, his legacy lives on throughout the city, from the iconic Erasmusbrug to the university named after him. Although he spent much of his life travelling, his influence remains deeply rooted in Rotterdam, inspiring a spirit of curiosity, knowledge, and open-mindedness.

Fred van Leer

Known for his bold style and witty personality, Fred van Leer is a popular Dutch TV presenter and fashion expert hailing from Rotterdam. He gained fame with shows like *Holland's Next Top Model* and *Say Yes to the Dress*. His larger-than-life presence and sharp sense of humour make him a household name, especially in Rotterdam, where he's a proud local.

Jandino Asporaat

Comedian and TV presenter Jandino Asporaat rose to fame with *De Dino Show*, a weekly programme featuring interviews with famous guests and comedic sketches, like the popular *FC Kip* fast-food series. His mix of humour and cultural commentary struck a chord with audiences. In 2023, Jandino expanded his brand by opening a real *FC Kip* restaurant in Rotterdam, which became a hit. Though born in Curacao, Rotterdam is his home and the heart of his creative journey.

Jules Deelder

Rotterdam's ultimate city poet — sharp, fast-talking, and always dressed in black. Born and raised here, Jules Deelder captured the soul of Rotterdam in his punchy, jazz-infused poetry, celebrating its resilience, humour, and no-nonsense attitude. A true night owl, he was a familiar face in the city's jazz clubs, often performing with his signature rapid-fire delivery. He died in 2019 shortly after his 75th birthday, but his words live on in street art, books, and the hearts of Rotterdammers who cherish his rebellious spirit.

↓ ERASMUS

↓ POEM BY JULES DEELDER

↓ REUS VAN ROTTERDAM, SEE PAGE 94

↓ DE ROTTERDAM BY REM KOOLHAAS

Lee Towers

A true Rotterdam icon, Lee Towers is the city's golden-voiced showman. Known for his deep love of Feyenoord, his songs *Mijn Feyenoord* and *You'll Never Walk Alone* have become anthems at De Kuip. Whenever Feyenoord wins a major trophy, he leads the victory celebrations in Coolsingel. For thirty years, he also sang *You'll Never Walk Alone* prior to the start of the Rotterdam Marathon, inspiring thousands of runners as they took on the challenge.

Neelie Kroes

A powerhouse in politics and business, Neelie Kroes made waves in both the Netherlands and wider Europe. Born and raised in Rotterdam, she carried the city's no-nonsense attitude into her career, from Dutch politics to the European Commission. As the EU's Competition Commissioner, she took on big tech and fought for fair markets. Her Rotterdam roots shaped her fearless leadership style, making her one of the most influential Dutch women in modern history.

Pim Fortuyn

Charismatic, controversial, and always outspoken, Pim Fortuyn was a politician who left a lasting mark on Rotterdam. A professor turned political leader, he shook up Dutch politics with his bold opinions and populist ideas. Rotterdam was his home and political base, where he resonated with the city's working-class spirit. His assassination in 2002 shocked the nation, but his influence on Dutch politics – and the city he loved – remains part of Rotterdam's modern history.

Rem Koolhaas

One of the world's most visionary architects, Rem Koolhaas has left a bold mark on Rotterdam. Born in the city, he founded OMA (Office for Metropolitan Architecture), shaping skylines worldwide. In his hometown, he designed De Rotterdam, the striking glass towers on the Wilhelminapier. His innovative, daring approach reflects Rotterdam's spirit – always forward-thinking, always reinventing itself. His influence stretches far beyond architecture, shaping urban design and modern cityscapes across the globe.

Robin van Persie

A Rotterdam football icon, Robin van Persie started his journey at Excelsior before rising through Feyenoord's ranks. At just 17, he helped Feyenoord win the 2002 UEFA Cup. After a legendary career with Arsenal and Manchester United, he returned home in 2018, scoring his 300th goal and lifting the KNVB Cup. A true local hero, he remains a Feyenoord favourite, inspiring future generations with his skill, passion, and deep connection to the city. And in March 2025, he came full circle – taking the reins as Feyenoord's manager.

Sevdaliza

Sevdaliza, an Iranian-born artist raised in Rotterdam, is known for her genre-defying sound, blending elements of trip-hop, R&B, and electronic music. A self-taught producer, she gained recognition with her debut album *ISON* in 2017. Her innovative art explores themes of identity, feminism, and body politics. Sevdaliza has built a global following, collaborating with artists like Grimes and Karol G and performing at festivals such as Coachella and Rock in Rio.

Waardenberg & De Jong

In the 1980s and 90s Waardenberg & De Jong were a legendary Dutch comedy duo known for their witty sketches, wordplay, and absurdist humour.

Their performances combined slapstick with social commentary, capturing the audience's attention in theatres. Although they stopped performing as a duo years ago, their clever dynamic and creativity, rooted in Rotterdam, still resonates with fans.

↓ FEYENOORD MUSEUM AT DE KUIP

FILMS & SERIES IN AND ABOUT ROTTERDAM

Who Am I? (1998)

Jackie Chan plays a secret agent who loses his memory after a mission goes wrong. Left stranded in Africa, he embarks on a thrilling journey to uncover his identity while being pursued by shadowy forces. With high-energy martial arts, daring stunts, and Jackie Chan's signature humour, the film sees him travel across continents, outsmarting enemies and piecing together his past. Featuring breathtaking action sequences, including the famous rooftop fight in Rotterdam, *Who Am I?* is a classic Jackie Chan adventure packed with adrenaline and fun.

De Marathon (2012)

A heartwarming Dutch comedy drama set in Rotterdam, following four out-of-shape mechanics struggling to keep their garage afloat. To raise money, they make a wild bet to run the Rotterdam Marathon. As they train, their friendships are tested, secrets come to light, and personal struggles unfold. Filled with humour, heart, and Rotterdam's working-class spirit, the film blends comedy with emotional depth, showing how determination and friendship can overcome life's toughest challenges.

De Liefhebbers (Shit Happens, 2019)

A Dutch drama about a family struggling to stay together. When their father, Jan, is diagnosed with Alzheimer's, his four grown children are forced to face their own problems and long-hidden secrets. As Jan's memory fades, tensions rise, and they must decide what really matters. Set in Rotterdam, this emotional film explores family bonds, love, and the challenges of dealing with change. A heartfelt story about how illness can test relationships but also bring people closer together.

Ome Cor (2022)

Another Rotterdam comedy-drama. The story follows Uncle Cor, an old dock worker caught committing benefits fraud. When he's exposed, he faces prison and risks losing his bond with his teenage daughter, Carola. Determined to make amends, he tries to turn his life around. The film features many famous actors and well-known Rotterdammers, adding to its local charm. Made on a tiny budget, most of the proceeds went to the Sophia Children's Hospital.

Hardcore Never Dies (2023)

This Dutch crime drama, set in 1990s Rotterdam, follows 17-year-old Michael, an aspiring pianist struggling with his music education. Seeking inspiration, his brother Danny introduces him to the city's emerging *gabber* music scene – a hardcore electronic genre. As Michael becomes immersed in this world of intense beats and brotherhood, he gets entangled in Danny's escalating drug business. Their involvement in the criminal underworld grows, forcing the brothers to fight for survival. The film showcases the vibrant *gabber* subculture and the challenges of balancing ambition with loyalty.

Santos (2023)

A gripping Rotterdam-set TV series about love, ambition, and crime. Glenn, an aspiring chef, and Yola, a non-profit entrepreneur, dream of a future together. But as Glenn gets pulled into drug dealing by his best friend, and Yola clashes with her ruthless, power-hungry mother, their love is tested. Caught between their ambitions and criminal ties, they struggle to stay together. With its raw storytelling, *Santos* became a hit, winning the Gouden Kalf for Best Television Series in 2023.

De Z van Zus (2024)

A heartwarming and humorous film about twin sisters Rianne and Juliette, who couldn't be more different. Rianne cares for their sick father and runs his snack bar in Rotterdam, while Juliette lives a glamorous life in Amsterdam. When their father dies, the sisters clash over his final wish to have his ashes scattered on the Spanish coast. Forced to go on a road trip together, the sisters must confront their differences and rediscover their bond.

Safe Harbor (2025)

A thrilling Rotterdam-based TV series created by Mark Williams, the creator of *Ozark*. The show follows a group of hackers who find themselves in over their heads after crossing paths with members of the Irish mob. They're hired to hack into the security system of Europe's largest shipping port, enabling undetected drug shipments to flow in and out. As they get deeper into the criminal underworld, their lives spiral out of control, leading to intense drama, betrayal, and dangerous consequences.

Drie dagen vis (2025)

Drie dagen vis tells the story of 68-year-old Gerrie, a retired bus driver living in the Algarve with his second wife, Rosa. Officially still registered in the Netherlands, he travels to Rotterdam once a year for routine check-ups. Staying with his Cape Verdean stepdaughter, he reunites with his troubled son, Dick, always hoping to spend quality time with him. However, this year, with Gerrie's health declining, their strained relationship is put to the test, and it may be his final visit to his home country.

BOOKS IN & ABOUT ROTTERDAM

Lord of the Flies – William Golding & Aimée de Jongh

Aimée de Jongh's graphic novel adaptation of *Lord of the Flies* brings a fresh, gripping take on William Golding's classic 1954 story. It follows a group of British schoolboys stranded on a deserted island, where survival turns into a brutal power struggle. De Jongh lives and works in Rotterdam. Her graphic novels have received critical acclaim and won dozens of awards, in the Netherlands, France, Japan, and the United States.

Terra Ultima – Raoul Deleo

Another brilliant illustrator from Rotterdam, Raoul Deleo, created *Terra Ultima*, a stunning book that takes readers on an adventure to a mysterious, undiscovered continent. Presented as a travel journal, it showcases breathtaking illustrations of fantastical creatures and landscapes, blending science and imagination. In 2022, the book was awarded the prestigious Gouden Penseel, a renowned Dutch jury prize for the best-illustrated children's book.

Exactitudes – Ari Versluis & Ellie Uyttenbroek

Exactitudes is a fascinating photography project by Rotterdam-based duo Ari Versluis and stylist Ellie Uyttenbroek, inspired by their interest in the dress codes of various social groups. They photograph people in identical poses and settings, offering a scientific overview of how humans strive to stand out by adopting group identities. This

exploration of individuality and uniformity has taken Versluis and Uyttenbroek around the world, from Rotterdam's streets to cities like Beijing, Rio de Janeiro, Casablanca, London, and Paris.

Character: A Novel of Father and Son – Ferdinand Bordewijk

This Dutch classic, set in pre-war Rotterdam, captures the city's tough, hardworking spirit. It follows the tense relationship between Jacob Katadreuffe, an ambitious young man, and his strict, ruthless father, Dreverhaven. Despite his father's harshness, Jacob fights to build a successful career in law. Written by proud Rotterdammer Ferdinand Bordewijk, the novel paints a vivid picture of the city's industrial past and was adapted into an Oscar-winning film.

The Ice-Cream Makers – Ernest van der Kwast

The Ice-Cream Makers by Rotterdam author Ernest van der Kwast follows Giovanni Talamini, a poet torn between his dreams and his family's ice-cream legacy. After leaving the family business to pursue poetry, Giovanni is called back home for help, forcing him to choose between tradition and his own path. Inspired by stories the author heard while visiting the owner of the Rotterdam ice-cream shop Venezia in his hometown in Northern Italy, this moving tale explores family, tradition, and personal ambition.

Shelter – Sanneke van Hassel

Nederzettingen by Rotterdam author Sanneke van Hassel is a collection of stories about finding a place to belong. The characters, from all corners of the world, have settled in the city, but some dream of an escape, for a weekend or to a completely new life. Four stories from *Nederzettingen* have been translated into English by Danny Guinan and are collected in the chapbook *Shelter*, which is published by Strangers Press in Norwich.

Taste of Rotterdam – Edwin Veekens

Love food? *Taste of Rotterdam* takes you on a culinary journey through the city's rich flavours and diverse culture. With stories from true Rotterdammers like Shirma Rouse, Tymon de Laat, and Sabine Biesheuvel, this cookbook offers a glimpse into the city's heart. Featuring local dishes from forty-one different countries, each recipe has a unique Rotterdam twist. It's a celebration of food, culture, and the people that make Rotterdam special.

Rotterdam Architecture City: The 100 Best Buildings

This is your ultimate guide to exploring Rotterdam's stunning architecture. It showcases one hundred of the city's best buildings, from modern masterpieces to hidden gems. It also points you to the best spots for dining in an architectural setting, entertainment, and cultural experiences, making it a must-read for architecture lovers.

Foto's – Vincent Mentzel

Vincent Mentzel is one of the most iconic Rotterdam-based photographers. For nearly forty years, he was the staff photographer for *NRC Handelsblad*, documenting major events from Dutch politics to global protests. His powerful portraits and intimate photo reports humanised politics for many readers. The photos in this book showcase his remarkable career, highlighting key moments in recent history, with contributions from notable writers (in Dutch only). A must-have for history and photography enthusiasts.

FUN FACTS

Nicknames

Rotterdam is a city of nicknames. Buildings, bridges, streets, and even neighbourhoods are given playful names, often even before construction begins. From iconic landmarks like *De Zwaan*, *De Hef*, and *De Kuip* to quirky ones like *Station Kapsalon*, *De Hoerenloper*, and *Hillywood*, Rotterdam has a nickname for almost everything. This tradition, which goes back a long way, has only grown stronger over time, partly because locals embraced it as part of their identity, turning it into a fun, self-affirming sport.

Stolpersteine

In the streets of Rotterdam, small brass plaques are embedded in the pavement. These are *Stolpersteine*, or 'stumbling stones', created to remember the victims of the Holocaust. Each plaque marks the last home or workplace of a Jewish person who was persecuted or killed during World War II. The aim is to encourage people to pause and reflect on these individuals' stories. These simple yet powerful markers help preserve Rotterdam's wartime history and remind us of the importance of tolerance and human rights.

Reus van Rotterdam

Rigardus Rijnhout, famous for his extraordinary height of 2.38 metres (the second-tallest Dutch person in history), was known as 'de Reus van Rotterdam'. Weighing 230 kilograms and with a shoe size of 62, Rijnhout's unusual size was caused by a growth disorder. He was known as a kind and gentle man, who

earned a living by renting himself out as a walking billboard. In 2011, a life-size statue of Rijnhout was placed in Wijkpark Het Oude Westen, close to where he grew up.

Football fever

Rotterdam lives and breathes football, with three professional clubs – a rarity in the Netherlands. Feyenoord, the most famous, has a rich history of national and international success, with its legendary stadium, De Kuip, at the heart of Dutch football culture. Sparta, the country's oldest professional club, has a deep-rooted tradition and develops young talent. Excelsior, based in Kralingen, also plays a key role in nurturing future stars. For Rotterdam fans, football is more than just a sport – it's a lifelong commitment. Once you pick a side, you're in it for life, fuelling fiercely passionate rivalries across the city.

Fountain takeover

Feyenoord fans have a legendary way of celebrating their victories. Whenever Feyenoord wins the championship or a cup final, thousands of fans rush to the city centre and jump into the Hofplein fountain. It's a wild, unforgettable scene – the smoke of red flares fills the air as fans celebrate in the water. The Hofplein fountain takeover is total madness and a true symbol of Rotterdam's deep passion for football.

Tasty invention

Did you know Rotterdam is the birthplace of the famous street-food dish *kapsalon*? This delicious fast-food meal – layers of fries, shawarma, melted cheese, salad, and garlic sauce – was created in the early 2000s at El Aviva, a shop in Delfshaven. It was first ordered by local hairdresser Nataniël 'Tati' Gomes, which is why it was named *kapsalon* (Dutch for 'hair salon'). El Aviva stopped trading, but *kapsalon* has spread far beyond Rotterdam and can now be found in Belgium, Germany, Suriname, and even Indonesia.

The World's Biggest Artwork

You might think that the largest artwork in the world is Michelangelo's Sistine Chapel ceiling. That's actually not the case. *The Horn of Plenty* in Rotterdam's Markthal covers over 11,000 m2 and is bigger than any other painted ceiling on the planet. Designed by Arno Coenen and Iris Roskam, this colourful masterpiece features giant images of fresh food sold in the market below, along with glimpses of the nearby Laurenskerk. This breathtaking piece of art transforms the Markthal into a modern masterpiece.

Brandgrens

De Brandgrens is a Rotterdam term that marks the boundary of the area devastated by the bombing of the city on 14 May 1940. To remember this event, lights have been embedded in the ground marking the fire boundary, each depicting flames, a Heinkel bomber, and Zadkine's *De Verwoeste Stad*. A 12-kilometre walking route follows *de Brandgrens*, offering visitors the chance to explore and reflect on the city's history.

PHOTO SPOTS

Markthal

Binnenrotte, 3011 PB
Stadsdriehoek (Centrum)

The Markthal is one of Rotterdam's top photo spots, thanks to its arched shape and stunning ceiling. For the best shot of the building, stand just outside on Binnenrotte, and centre the archway in your frame to capture its full scale. Inside, aim your camera upwards to snap the colourful artwork in all its glory. For a dynamic angle, try shooting from the entrance, where the curve of the building frames the bustling market.

Kubuswoningen

Overblaak, 3011 TA
Stadsdriehoek (Centrum)

The Cube Houses are not to be missed either, thanks to their bold design and striking angles. The tilted cubes create a surreal, almost futuristic vibe – perfect for eye-catching shots. For the best angle, stand in the central courtyard and look up for a dramatic geometric frame. Shoot from below to capture the cubes towering above for a street view. Sunset makes the yellow pop even more.

Erasmusbrug

Leuvehoofd, 3011 XT
Stadsdriehoek (Centrum)

Another must-see for photographers in Rotterdam is Erasmusbrug, with its sleek, modern design making it a standout subject for any photographer. From Leuvehoofd, head to the waterfront for the perfect shot, with Rem Koolhaas's De Rotterdam as a

↓ DEPOT BOIJMANS VAN BEUNINGEN

striking backdrop. The bridge just asks to be photographed, and a low angle shot makes it look even more dramatic.

Depot Boijmans Van Beuningen

Mathenesserlaan/ Rochussenstraat, 3015 CX Dijkzigt (Centrum)

From the crossing of Mathenesserlaan and Rochussenstraat, you can get a striking shot of Depot Boijmans Van Beuningen. Its spectacular mirrored, bowl-shaped design stands out against the cityscape, reflecting the sky as well as the surrounding trees and buildings for a stunning effect. This spot gives you the perfect angle to capture the Depot in all its beauty, making it a top photo spot for anyone who loves architecture.

Little C

Coolhaven 1, 3015 GC Dijkzigt (Centrum)

From the pathway in front of the Deense Zeemanskerk in Coolhaven, you have a fantastic view of the residential Little C complex. This spot lets you capture its unique mix of modern and industrial-style architecture, with brick façades, metal bridges, and large windows creating a New York-inspired vibe. Frame your shot with the water in the foreground to add depth to your image.

Wilhelminapier

Westerkade, 3016 CM Scheepvaartkwartier (Centrum)

The view of Wilhelminapier is another great shot, with its mix of modern skyscrapers and historic buildings creating a stunning skyline. From Westerkade, position yourself near the waterfront for a perfect panoramic angle. Shoot during the golden hour for the best lighting or try a long exposure at night to capture the city lights reflecting on the water – guaranteed to make your photos stand out.

Kralingse Plas

Plaszoom, 3062 CL Kralingse Bos (Kralingen-Crooswijk)

At the northeastern corner of Kralingse Plas, near restaurant De Schone Lei, you'll find a wooden walkway over the water – one of the best spots for a stunning photo. From here, you can capture the beauty of Kralingse Plas with Rotterdam's skyline rising in the background. The contrast between nature and the city makes for a spectacular shot.

Skyline

Maaskade, 3071 NJ Noordereiland (Feijenoord)

For one of the best skyline shots of Rotterdam, head to Maaskade on Noordereiland. From here, you'll have a perfect panoramic view of the city, with the towering high-rises on Boompjes all in one frame. Plus, at the eastern tip of Noordereiland, on Prins Hendrikkade, you can capture an epic shot of the iconic Hef, a striking piece of Rotterdam's history.

Hotel New York

Koninginnenhoofd, 3072 AD Kop van Zuid (Feijenoord)

Hotel New York is a picture-perfect location, with its historic charm standing out against the sleek high-rises of Wilhelminapier. The best spot to photograph it is from Koninginnenhoofd, where you get a clear view of the building framed by the skyline. From here, you can capture the striking contrast between old and new architecture, with the historic hotel set against the modern Port of Rotterdam and Montevideo buildings.

Fenix

Koninginnenhoofd,
3072 AD Kop van Zuid
(Feijenoord)

While you're at Koninginnenhoofd, don't forget to turn around and snap a photo of Fenix too. This museum, inside the renovated Fenixloods II, you'll find a cool mix of old and new design. Its twisting Tornado staircase is a real showstopper, with smooth curves that seem to defy gravity. The spiral shape and flowing lines make it a seriously eye-catching photo.

↓ HOTEL NEW YORK

BREAKFAST

By Jarmusch

Goudsesingel 64, 3011 KD Stadsdriehoek (Centrum); Nieuwe Binnenweg 575, 3023 EP Nieuwe Westen (Delfshaven), byjarmusch.nl

An American breakfast never gets old, especially when prepared by By Jarmusch. Have a sweet tooth? Their French toast with fresh blueberries and blueberry compote won't disappoint. They serve breakfast all day long, for those who like a lie-in.

Louise Petit Déjeuner

Veerhaven 12B, 3016 CJ Scheepvaartkwartier (Centrum), louisepetitrestaurant.com

Bonjour! While the interior of Louise Petit Déjeuner is mesmerising, their menu is even better. The delicious *crêpe comté et truffle* and *croque madame* will keep you coming back. In the evening, the restaurant transforms to a fancy place to wine and dine *à la France*.

Parqiet

Baden Powelllaan 20, 3016 GJ Scheepvaartkwartier (Centrum), parqiet.com

Imagine sitting on a lovely terrace, surrounded by greenery, with a healthy plate or bowl in front of you. At Parqiet this becomes reality. Here, you'll enjoy a falafel flatbread, with a cinnamon roll and cappuccino on the side. Does it get any better?

Man met Bril Koffie

Vijverhofstraat 70, 3032 SN Agniesebuurt (Noord), Linker Rottekade 12, 3034 RD, manmetbrilkoffie.nl

For everyone who's looking for a *'bakkie pleur'* — what Rotterdammers call an excellent cup of coffee — this is the place. Take a seat and sip on one of their fair-trade coffees, while finishing work or reading the newspaper. Be there before

10am to enjoy their breakfast plate.

Arzu

Bergweg 209A, 3037EJ Oude Noorden (Noord), arzurotterdam.nl

This stylish café is all about pancakes and coffee. You'll also find other meals on the menu, but why would you? The apple pie, red velvet, and banana caramel pancakes are the best. Don't forget to grab one of their handmade food bars on the way home. You won't regret it.

COFFEE SPOTS

Nine Bar

Botersloot 44a, 3011 HH Stadsdriehoek (Centrum), nine-bar.com

Everyone who loves to start their morning with the newspaper on the right and a cup of coffee on the left, should visit the small, homely Nine Bar. Once you sit down, you won't be able to resist their pistachio cookies or carrot cake. Yum!

Social

Herenplaats 1, 3011 LP Stadsdriehoek (Centrum), socialrotterdam.nl

The living-room vibe, art on the walls, and tasty menu (their New York pastrami sandwich is on fire!) will make you think about your next visit. For the busy bees in town: their Grab & Go window serves an excellent cup of coffee within a few minutes.

NICE

Hoogstraat 42, 3011 PR Stadsdriehoek (Centrum), @nice.neighbourhood

We love a cosy, aesthetic coffee spot. And luckily, there are tons of them in Rotterdam. One that really stands out is NICE. You can tell their coffee is made by talented baristas. Their sandwiches are around 12 euros, but worth every penny.

↓ PIZZA AT OLD SCUOLA, STADSDRIEHOEK (CENTRUM)

Coppi

Bergweg 316, 3032 BB Agniesebuurt (Noord), coppikoffie.nl

At COPPI, they fix your bike, sell biking gear, and even organise rides for die-hard cycling fans. But when you're not that into cycling, the staff will welcome you with open arms as well. Good to know: it's a laptop-friendly place.

Bonza Koffie

Zomerhofstraat 71, 3032 CK Agniesebuurt (Noord), bonzakoffie.nl

This spot is what we call a hidden gem. You can find Bonza Koffie in Noord, in a street you could easily walk past. But that won't happen, thanks to the smell of their coffee, kimchi toasts and carrot cakes. They just grab your attention and make you order. Sorry not sorry.

Urban Espresso Bar

Nieuwe Binnenweg 263, 3021 GD Middelland (Delfshaven), urbanespressobar.nl

On your way to the Urban Espresso Bar, you'll cross the hectic streets of Rotterdam West. Once you enter this vibrant place, the long table filled with laptops, cappuccinos and freshly baked croissants will welcome you. Their sunny outdoor space is lovely to enjoy a beer on while you work on that tan.

BAKERIES

Dudok

Meent 88, 3011 JP Stadsdriehoek (Centrum), Baden Powelllaan 12, 3016 GJ Scheepvaartkwartier (Centrum), dudok.nl

In 1991, Café Brasserie Dudok opened its doors. To attract customers, the owners decided to bake some apple pies. Little did they know that from ten pies a day they'd end up baking thousands.

Harvest Café & Bakery

Glashaven 107, 3011 XG Stadsdriehoek (Centrum), harvestcafeandbakery.com

Delicious coffee and freshly baked goods? Go to Harvest Café & Bakery. Originally from Melbourne, Australia, Harvest brings lots of flavour. They serve a wonderful breakfast, and their bakery is amazing. Sourdough? Of course. *Canelé*? Yes, please. *Pain au chocolat*? Can't wait.

Koekela

Nieuwe Binnenweg 79A, 3014 GE Oude Westen (Centrum), koekela.nl

When you have to queue for cake, you know it's good. At Koekela, they have more than proven themselves over the years: they have been part of Rotterdam since 2003. And we hope they'll never stop. Make sure to get a piece of their Chocolate truffle mousse cake during your stay.

Jordy's Bakery Rotterdam

jordysbakery.nl

This no-nonsense bakery can be found at four locations and is the best place to go for sourdough. Their breads come in all kinds of sizes, colours and flavours. After all these years, founder Jordy still finds happiness in baking his loaves, while his wife Marieke shares this passion in serving their customers who eat in. A dream team, to say the least.

Le Petit Jean

Nieuwe Binnenweg 174, 3015 BJ Oude Westen (Centrum), insta @ lepetitejeanrotterdam

Owner Maurice Petitjean warms our hearts with his pistachio croissants, éclairs, and mini tarts. And his 14K Instagram followers feel the same way. You can find his creations in Oude Westen. So go for a stroll through the city and treat yourself to some Le Petit Jean magic.

Bakkit

Zwaanshals 299, 3035 KH Oude Noorden (Noord), bakkit.nl

You'll find Bakkit in Noord. The perfect spot to take a little break from a shopping spree (there are lots of vintage shops in the area). When we tell you that the team includes the winner of the Dutch TV show *Heel Holland Bakt* as well as a world class pastry chef, you know you're in the right place.

BRUNCH & LUNCH

Guliano

guliano.it

Make your way to one of Guliano's branches for Italian sandwiches. Everything on their menu is delicious, but the sandwich with thinly sliced rare beef rib, parmesan, and truffle mayonnaise stands out. The queue is worth it.

Little Italy

Lombardkade 51a, 3011 ZD Stadsdriehoek (Centrum), insta @little_italy_rotterdam

Little Italy in the city centre offers the best of two Italian worlds. Besides their delicious pizzas and sandwiches, they also sell Italian products to take home. Made with love and available at a fair price.

Wolly

Noordplein 1, 3035 EA Oude Noorden (Noord), wollyaandewaterkant.nl

We love Noordplein! It was already booming – especially with Rotterdamse Oogst market on Saturdays – but since Wolly has entered the game, it's been wild out there. Take a seat at their sunny space by the water or grab a table inside in one of their diner booths, and discover something new.

Staten Café

Statenweg 134D, 3039 JM Blijdorp (Noord), statencafe.nl

Just behind Central Station, you'll find the family-focused neighbourhood Blijdorp. It has a very peaceful vibe compared to the busy city centre. Luckily, Staten Café is there to shake things up. Their enticing menu – with happy hour breakfast – takes its job very seriously.

On Other Drugs

Bergse Rechter Rottekade 1, 3051 AB Hillegersberg (Schiebroek), onotherdrugs.nl

Anyone who owns a boat, has a love for aesthetics, and a craving for sunshine should gather at On Other Drugs. Their intimate sunny outdoor space is filled with comfy bean bags. A dreamy spot if you want to enjoy your summer to the fullest. And yes, you can dock your boat right there.

Bun

Nieuwe Binnenweg 256B, 3021 GP Middelland (Delfshaven), bunrotterdam.nl

If a place is always crowded and customers walk out with a smile, you know they must be doing something right. At Bun, our wildest dreams came true – sandwich-wise, that is. Their tuna melt is crazy. But be sure to check their website, as they tend to sell out – especially on weekends.

De Bonte Keukentafel

Kromme Zandweg 102, 3084 ND Zuiderpark (Charlois), debontekeukentafel.nl

At De Bonte Keukentafel, not just the brownies, goat's cheese sandwiches, and chai lattes warm your heart. Their staff do a pretty good job as well. In partnership with Stichting Bont, people with learning disabilities get a chance to cook and serve here. And they love it.

RDM Kantine

Heijplaatstraat 3, 3089JB Heijplaat (Charlois), rdmkantine.nl

Having lunch in a historical building while enjoying the stunning views of the Rotterdam harbour: it's possible at RDM Kantine. Formerly used by industrial workers, it is accessible to everyone now. The low prices make the sandwiches, salads, and soups taste even better.

FRIES & SNACKS

Bram Ladage

bramladage.nl

Some places become city icons. One of them is Bram Ladage. They opened in Rotterdam in 1965, and people have been obsessed ever since. You'll now find their branches all over town. Their red and blue logo will grab your attention, and their crispy fries leave a lasting impression.

Drippy's Burgers

insta @drippysburgers

Owned by influencer Kaj Gorgels and adored by fast-food lovers in and around Rotterdam: Drippy's Burgers serves grass-fed beef and halal burgers. Our favourite is the brioche bun with melted cheddar, crunchy white onion and pickles.

Frietboutique

frietboutique.nl

The best way to celebrate moments is with fries, snacks, and ice cream, right? At Frietboutique, they know how to throw a tasty party. That's what they've been doing for almost ten years now. You'll find them all over Rotterdam.

Pomms

Coolsingel 107b, 3012 AG Cool (Centrum), pomms.nl

You'll find Pomms in the heart of the city. They arrived in 2014 and never left. Lucky us. Try a *kroket*, a popular Dutch deep-fried snack with a ragout filling. Or have their fries with *pindasaus* (peanut sauce). You won't regret it.

THE GOAT

Schiedamse Vest 14, 3011 BA Stadsdriehoek (Centrum), insta @thegoat_nl

At THE GOAT all your fastfood dreams will come true. Smash burgers, a plate full of nachos, strawberry milkshakes, waffles, loaded fries … The list keeps going; just go there and experience it yourself.

Maaskantine

Plantagelaan 2, 3063 NG De Esch (Kralingen-Crooswijk), demaaskantine.nl

When the sun's out and the temperatures rise above twenty degrees, we always hurry to Maaskantine. This pop-up restaurant — yes, they're only open in summer — is the perfect spot whenever you crave a beer and a burger in the sun.

DINNER

Little V

Grotekerkplein 109, 3011 GC Stadsdriehoek (Centrum), littlev.nl

The flavours of Little V's recipes bring you to the south of Vietnam. Or should we say: heaven on earth? Decide for yourself after you've tried their chef's special four-course menu. They won't disappoint.

Kiiro

Inside the Markthal, 3011 GZ Stadsdriehoek (Centrum), kiiro.nl

Move over Indian or Thai curries … Immerse yourself in Japanese curries at Kiiro, the first restaurant in the Netherlands to serve these delicious dishes. The beauty of Japan is just around the corner from Markthal. One *chikin shīzu*, please.

Supermercado

Schiedamse Vest 91, 3012 BG Cool (Centrum), supermercadorotterdam.com

A restaurant with a Mexican, Brazilian or Peruvian twist is always at the top of our list. Is there anyone who gets bored of tacos, ceviche or cheesy nachos? At Supermercado, the vibe is always bubbly. Try one of their cocktails and let the party begin.

Hung Kee

Witte de Withstraat 61B, 3012 BM Cool (Centrum)

Craving some Asian food while strolling through the heart of Rotterdam? Hung Kee is located in one of the busiest streets of the city and surrounded by bars. Make sure you drop by for some *gado-gado* or *chop suey* before you start drinking the night away.

Warung Mini

Witte de Withstraat 47, 3012 BM Cool (Centrum), warungmini.com

About 35 years ago, a man and a woman had one mission: introducing the locals of Rotterdam to the flavours of Indonesian, Javanese, and Surinamese cuisine. An ongoing effort, but after their pulled chicken roti, we're sure you will be hooked.

Bazaar

Witte de Withstraat 16, 3012 BP Cool (Centrum), hotelbazaar.nl

Those who make their way to Witte de Withstraat will sooner or later notice Bazaar's vibrant outside space and colourful interior. It's a popular spot, to say the least. People come here for their international vibe and diverse menu. *The Royal Persian lamb* and *mosàmma* make our hearts melt every time.

Tai Wu

Mauritsweg 24-26, 3012 JR Cool (Centrum), taiwu.sitedish.shop

Take a seat at Tai Wu for Chinese Cantonese cuisine. Their portions are big and the flavours incredible. You might need to wait for a bit, but as they say, all good things take time.

Burgertrut

Delftseplein 39, 3013 AA CS-kwartier (Centrum), roodkapje.org

Vegan burgers, veggie burgers, and organic burgers: at Burgertrut they want everyone – regardless of their diet – to enjoy the flavours of the world's favourite fast-food snack. Within walking distance of Central Station, so once you arrive in Rotterdam, you know what you have to do.

Sranang

West-Kruiskade 2A, 3014 AP Oude Westen (Centrum), sranangrotterdam.nl

People have been finding their way to Sranang for more than forty years. The dishes they serve in their Chinese Surinamese restaurant are not only mouthwatering, but also affordable. This is your place for *roti*, *moksi meti*, *saoto* and a variety of rolls.

Kiem Foei

West-Kruiskade 29b, 3014 AK Oude Westen (Centrum), kiemfoei.nl

The most mouthwatering dishes are often made in not-so-fancy places. The interior at Kiem Foei is very basic, but their menu with Surinamese and Antillean dishes is far from it. We love their rolls with *pom*, a Surinamese oven dish made from the root vegetable *pomtayer*.

Soi3

West-Kruiskade 63a, 3014 AM Oude Westen (Centrum), soi3.nl

Anyone craving Thai food should run to Soi3. Some people say their classic *phad Thai* tastes exactly as it would in Thailand. Decide for yourself.

Café Marseille

1e Middellandstraat 16B, 3014 BD Oude Westen (Centrum), cafemarseille.nl

Joie de vivre at the Southern French bistro Café Marseille. Shrimps, lobster, mussels: any fish enthusiasts will leave with a full belly. The seventy seats inside create a cosy vibe. On Sundays, they serve oysters for only 2 euros: hard to resist.

↓ CAFÉ MARSEILLE

↓ MASA

Masa

's-Gravendijkwal 140D, 3015 CC Oude Westen (Centrum), masa-bar.com

Hello, Mexico lovers! Masa is a little present from us to you. When you unwrap it, you'll find a menu filled with seasonal, local ingredients, plant-based options, and some Mexican vibes. And not only is their food worth mentioning, their cocktail bar is amazing too.

Le Souq

Voorhaven 54B, 3024 RP Delfshaven-Schiemond (Delfshaven), lesouqdelfshaven.nl

A Lebanese restaurant: what's not to like? The colourful and tasty menu has something for everyone, from vegetarian to meat lover. Surprise yourself with the *Le Souq Mix* or enjoy their different mezze, *labneh*, *fatoush* or *sambousik*. The choices are endless.

Bar Pulpo

Scheepstimmermanslaan 15A, 3016 AC Scheepvaartkwartier (Centrum), barpulpo.nl

A seafood bar in an Instagrammable setting. That's Bar Pulpo. Everything on the menu is cooked to order in their charcoal oven. Being in the restaurant feels like chilling with friends in their living room, but with a very talented chef in the background.

De Ballentent

Parkkade 1, 3016 GN Scheepvaartkwartier (Centrum), deballentent.nl

Everyone – literally everyone – in Rotterdam knows De Ballentent. Not for their stylish interior, but for the warm atmosphere and their signature meatballs – plain, with fries or with bread. We'd recommend booking, because lots of locals and tourists want to experience their low-priced meals.

De Machinist aan de Cool

Willem Buytewechstraat 45, 3024 BK Cool (Centrum), demachinist.nl

If you want to have a summer night with your feet in the sand, have a big celebration with a fancy dinner or play volleyball with your friends: at De Machinist aan de Cool, the possibilities are endless. So, grab your friends and move to this hidden gem in Rotterdam West.

Klaargemaakt

Schiekade 770, 3032 AL Agniesebuurt (Noord), klaargemaakt.nl

From texture to colours and taste: the chefs at Klaargemaakt love to work their magic in the kitchen. And all that love goes into their flavours. Most people order a few small plates to share. We're big fans of their feta cream with beetroot. A big bonus is their sunny outdoor space, which lots of restaurants lack.

Station Bergweg

Bergweg 335, 3037 EP Bergpolder (Noord), stationbergweg.nl

Sometimes our heart makes a little jump. When we first walked into Station Bergweg, it jumped a bit higher. The industrial building is filled with different counters representing different kitchens (Italian, Spanish, Japanese), and the vibe is low-key and relaxed. You can also grab a drink or two, three ...

Silbar

Bergweg 94A, 3036 BE Liskwartier (Noord), silbar-rotterdam.nl

Tacos, antojitos, tortas, postres ... Going to Silbar feels like stepping into a slice of Mexico, located in the north of Rotterdam. Tip: feel like spicing up your Tuesday night? Their Taco Tuesdays are something else, especially with the sun on your face and a cocktail in your hand.

Bar Dertien

Linker Rottekade 13, 3034 NT Oude Noorden (Noord), insta @bardertien

Enjoying fresh and local ingredients, natural wines, peaceful surroundings — Hello, Rotte, birds and blossoming trees — that's why people go to Bar Dertien. This aesthetic spot is one of those places that keep your attention for hours and hours. Especially after the first bite.

Rottiedam

Oostzeedijk 356-a, 3063 CD Kralingen (Kralingen-Crooswijk), rottiedam.nl

Roti rolls or *roti* dishes: whatever kind you like, Rottiedam has it. The Nepalese owner worked his way up from kitchen assistant to king of *roti*. And if the Dutch chef Herman den Blijker stops by, you know it's worth a try.

Hotel New York

Koninginnenhoofd 1, 3072 AD Kop van Zuid (Feijenoord), hotelnewyork.nl

You can find one of Rotterdam's most famous restaurants in the former head office of the Holland America Line. Dining at Hotel New York means a unique experience, history all around, and *vitello tonnato*, coquilles or vegetarian burgers.

21 pinchos Fenix

Nico Koomanskade 1024, 3072 LM Katendrecht (Feijenoord), 21pinchos.nl

Imagine picnic tables by the water, a pink sky after sunset, and some tapas in front of you. At 21 pinchos Fenix, the lovely staff creates a vibrant Spanish afternoon just like that, with or without sangria. *Buen provecho!*

Matroos en het meisje

Delistraat 52, 3072 ZL Katendrecht (Feijenoord), dematroosenhetmeisje.nl

This is a restaurant to take a date, a very good friend or your mum. The chequered tablecloths, paintings on the wall, and candles on the table create a celebratory setting. And that's what they do best at Matroos en het meisje: celebrating life. With their four-course menu, for example.

Paviljoen aan het Water

Brielselaan 157, 3081 AC Tarwewijk (Charlois), paviljoenaanhetwater.com

Keep an eye out for this one, because Paviljoen aan het Water only opens their doors for summer. This pop-up restaurant serves delicious food in combination with an exhibition, performance or film screening. Once you arrive, it feels like you step into a cosy living room.

Yokohama Ramen Saito

Parkweg 406, 3119 CV Nieuwland (Schiedam), insta @yokohamaramensaito

When you're looking for a good, tasty bowl of ramen, Yokohama Ramen Saito is the place. It's located in Schiedam, just a few minutes by metro from Rotterdam's city centre. And after one bite of their homemade ramen, you will make that journey over and over again.

↓ STATION BERGWEG

BRING THE PARENTS

Bar Bù

Van Vollenhovenstraat 19, 3016 BG Scheepvaartkwartier (Centrum), bar-bu.nl

At Bar Bù, you'll find Chinese dishes with a touch of French flair. Add a Japanese whisky and you have the best of three worlds. They care not just about feeding the body, but nourishing the soul too. And that is what they do best at this stunning restaurant.

Tres

Vijf Werelddelen 75, 3071 PS Kop van Zuid (Feijenoord), tresrotterdam.com

The Dutch chef Michael van der Kroft takes you on a culinary journey with techniques from all over the world. Once you take a seat, he'll tell you all about the farmers and artisans who help create the most beautiful and delicious dishes. Warning: they only seat twelve.

Vislocale Kaap

Delistraat 48c, 3072 ZL Katendrecht (Feijenoord)

Take your veggie- and fish-loving friends to Vislocale Kaap and spoil yourself. The restaurant is owned by Emmy Baris, who is married to gastronomy icon and well-known restaurateur Rob Baris. We love it all, from the fresh fish to the laid-back atmosphere and the French interior. A must-go if you're into *fruits de mer*.

Rijntje

Prinses Margrietlaan 93a, 3051 Hillegersberg (Hillegersberg-Schiebroek), rijntjerotterdam.nl

A small restaurant but with a great kitchen. We love the super-friendly staff as much as the food. French classics in a bright atmosphere and great outdoor seating close to the River Rotte as a bonus.

GOING OUT

WINE & COCKTAILS

Botanero

Mariniersweg 55, 3011 NE Stadsdriehoek (Centrum), insta @botanerorotterdam

This is another classic that can't be missed. Botanero was picked by Gault & Milau in 2022, when they received the title Best Cocktail Bar of the Netherlands. That sets the bar for the weekend! The drink Chanclas Mexicanas keeps calling us.

Café Verward

Hoogstraat 69A, 3011 PH Stadsdriehoek (Centrum), insta @cafeverward

Crave a dry, fruity, spicy or buttery glass of white wine? At Café Verward, the staff asks you to tell them your wishes, and they will make sure your dreams come true. They don't have a menu, so your evening is in their hands. Magic hands.

Wijnbar het Eigendom

Witte de Withstraat 45B, 3012 BM Cool (Centrum), heteigendom.nl

Combine great wines and music with one of the busiest streets of Rotterdam, and you'll find Wijnbar het Eigendom. No matter the time of year, this place is always crowded. Small sidenote: was chosen as the best wine bar in the Netherlands in 2017.

The Rumah

Oude Binnenweg 110C, 3012 JG Cool (Centrum), insta @therumahrotterdam

'A Neighbourhood Cocktail Pub', that's how The Rumah loves to present themselves. And to be honest, it is the reason why we love them so much. Here you sip on some cocktails (possibly the best of 2024, according to Gault & Milau) and have keep chatting for hours and hours.

Amehoela

Lijnbaan 40, 3012 EP Cool (Centrum), amehoela-rotterdam.nl

Cocktails that not only taste like they're from heaven but also look like a dream come true. The bartenders at Amehoela know how to catch our eye with their cocktails. Besides their little pieces of art (do try the Soul Healer), they also serve wine and champagne.

Spikizi

Zwarte Paardenstraat 91a, 3012 VK Cool (Centrum), insta @spikizibar

Places where they don't take reservations but keep spontaneity alive and well are our favourites. Cocktailbar Spikizi is located just around the corner from the busy Witte de Withstraat. So, head down there, order an espresso martini, and play a board game for a night full of fun.

OX Rotterdam

Schiekade 189, 3013 BR CS-kwartier (Centrum), insta @oxrotterdam

Do you feel like taking your date night to the next level? Then the contemporary Chinese restaurant & cocktail bar OX is the place to be. The dimmed lights, candlelight, and one-of-a-kind menu make it an evening to remember. Note: once you enter the building, it can take a bit of searching to find the bar.

La Soirée

Veerhaven 12B, 3016 CJ Scheepvaartkwartier (Centrum), insta @barlasoiree

Maybe one of Rotterdam's best kept secrets is cocktail bar La Soirée. Once you pass the red curtains, a whole new world opens: a world full of fancy cocktails and a romantic atmosphere. The perfect spot to get into the weekend spirits with a Moscow mule. Just saying.

Le Nord

Proveniersstraat 33a, 3033 CA Provenierswijk (Noord), lenord.nl

Within a one-minute walk from Rotterdam Central Station, you'll enter Proveniersstraat, a calm street filled with 1930s houses and a few popular bars. One of them is Le Nord, famous for its delicious wines, cheese platters, and laid-back outdoor seating area.

Walsjerot

Bentinckplein 5, 3039 KL Blijdorp (Noord), walsjerot.nl

Not sure which wine to choose? At Walsjerot they make any doubts disappear like clouds on a sunny day. They have more than seventy open wine bottles available, from which you can try a sip or (half) a glass. Let's find your new favourite!

↓ CAFÉ DE SCHOUW

Juni

Oostzeedijk 340A, 3063 CC Kralingen (Kralingen-Crooswijk), insta @junirotterdam

Once you set foot in the Netherlands, a visit to a cheese bar is non-negotiable. Luckily, at Juni they serve more than a fine collection of cheeses. They also have some amazing wines on the menu. The restaurant has space for just twenty guests, so be there on time.

BEER

Proeflokaal Reijngoud

Schiedamse Vest 148, 3011 BG Stadsdriehoek (Centrum) proeflokaalreijngoud.nl

When a place has two branches in the city of Rotterdam, it means that people really love what they do. Both have multiple draught beers (from 28 to 40) and over two hundred bottled varieties. So, prepare yourself for a night full of good drinks and laughs at Proeflokaal Reijngoud.

Bokaal

Nieuwemarkt 11, 3011 HP Stadsdriehoek (Centrum), bokaalrotterdam.nl

After a workday, Bokaal is where you want to grab a table and relax. Both their big outdoor space and warm interior bring smiles on faces. As does their menu filled with over seventy beers to choose from. Their location in the heart of Rotterdam is the icing on the cake.

Café de Schouw

Witte de Withstraat 80, 3012 BT Cool (Centrum), insta @cafedeschouw

No matter the day, at Café de Schouw it's always party time. Seriously: they even turn a dull Monday evening into something spicy. So, who's ordering the first round of beers tonight? We promise that the atmosphere will have you and your friends dancing the night away.

Café de Witte Aap

Witte de Withstraat 78, 3012 BS Cool (Centrum), dewitteaap.nl

Café de Witte Aap is a true gem in the city centre, with their selection of over seventy bottled beers, DJs who know how to get the dance floor going, and board games to break the ice. One thing is for sure: after a night here, you'll go home with some wild stories to tell.

Bierboutique

Witte de Withstraat 40B, 3012 BR Cool (Centrum), insta @bierboutiquerotterdam

With more than ninety flavours in the house, Bierboutique will definitely be your cup of tea — or beer, actually. In the evening, this place becomes a vibrant spot to shake your hips and sing along to some upbeat tunes. Anyone who wants to spoil their taste buds and give dancing a go: Bierboutique is for you.

Kaapse Maria

Mauritsweg 52, 3012 JW Cool (Centrum), kaapsemaria.nl

Ciders, beers, (natural) wines, and meals that change with the seasons. At gastropub Kaapse Maria you'll find everything for a night out. Their wooden, warm interior will make you feel at home within seconds. Especially important if you're planning to catch up for hours.

Biergarten

Schiestraat 18, 3013 BR CS-kwartier (Centrum), biergartenrotterdam.nl

What is a city without a biergarten? Not much of one … Luckily, Rotterdam is blessed with one of the coolest of them all. During summertime, everyone gathers at this spot, orders a beer (or something else) and catches up with friends — or dances their arse off.

Café Steijn

Nieuwe Binnenweg 345B, 3021 GJ Middelland (Delfshaven), cafesteijn.com

Once you sit down at Café Steijn, we assure you that you'll feel relaxed at this laid-back restaurant and bar or its sunny outdoor space. Combine their extensive drinks menu (beers, G&Ts, and wines) with one of their burgers or some fried snacks.

Bakkeliet

Nieuwe Binnenweg 328C, 3021 GV Middelland (Delfshaven), cafebakeliet.nl

This easy-going bar brings together people who love beer, vinyl, and electronic music. You'll find them at the cosiest corner in Rotterdam West, where you can enjoy a drink or two with a view of a green park by the water, while watching the world — and the locals — go by.

Keilecafé

Vierhavensstraat 46-50, 3029 BG Bospolder-Tussendijken (Delfshaven), keilecafe.nl

Craving a vintage shopping session, some house vibes to dance to or a sunny afternoon with beer and pizza? At Keilecafé you can have it all for the summer. They even have an open-air cinema, karaoke sessions, and games.

QUEER

Keerweer

Keerweer 14, 3012 KB Cool (Centrum), insta @keerweer

Having been around for 35+ years, gay bar Keerweer belongs to Rotterdam like no other. What to expect? Fun events — often hosted by the most amazing drag queens — lots of Dutch music, and Rotterdam humour. Just go in for a beer or two.

Ferry's

Westblaak 127, 3012 KJ Cool (Centrum), ferryrotterdam.nl

We love some queer vibes. Ferry's is the place to find them. On weekends, the LGBT+ community gathers here to dance the night away while the speakers drop hits from Beyoncé, Destiny's Child or the Sugababes. Tip: Thursday is karaoke night.

CLUBS

Rotown

Nieuwe Binnenweg 19, 3014 GB Oude Westen (Centrum), rotown.nl

Order a pizza, sip on a beer, and sing along with the variety of alternative artists that climb the Rotown stage. Every Friday and Saturday night, this bar turns into a club. Not a crazy and loud club that draws the masses — think of an intimate, relaxed, and local vibe.

Annabel

Schiestraat 20, 3013 AH CS-kwartier (Centrum), annabel.nu

Dancing in your own little bubble during a silent disco, singing along to famous artists, or moving your hips to popular hits: at Annabel, you can do it all. Their calendar is always filled with exciting events.

Perron

Schiestraat 42, 3013 AH CS-kwartier (Centrum), perron.nl

You heard it right: another techno spot in Rotterdam. But Perron is not like any other. The dance hall strikes a balance between intimacy and spaciousness, with a dark atmosphere that still feels warm and inviting. They know exactly which artists to invite for your electronic heart to beat a little faster. So, what will you be wearing?

160K

Schiekade 201, 3013 BR CS-kwartier (Centrum), insta @160k_rotterdam

With the COVID pandemic leaving the owner with a 160k debt, he came up with the idea for this retro arcade hall and pizza bar. Here's a fun detail: a sign above the entrance shows how much of the debt has been paid off day after day. Who's up for a game and a slice? *Every little helps.*

BIRD

Raampoortstraat 24, 3032 AH Agniesebuurt (Noord), bird-rotterdam.nl

Chances are that if you ask locals about their favourite Rotterdam club, they'll come up with BIRD. There's always something going on: from nights of electronic music to R&B, urban, and dancehall pumping through the speakers … BIRD is all about inclusion, community, and good times.

MONO

Vijverhofstraat 15, 3032 SB Agniesebuurt (Noord), insta @mono_rotterdam

Creativity all around. At MONO, creative souls come together to dance and connect. The sound is mostly focused on techno and house. Because of the intimate vibe, you'll connect easily with the other party peeps. Just give it a try and discover both established and upcoming artists.

Toffler

Weena-Zuid 33, 3012 NH Cool (Centrum), toffler.nl

Grooving to techno beats or house tunes is done best at the underground techno club Toffler. The DJ booth has been occupied by a number of international as well as Dutch talents. Take the stairs down to the dark room and dance the night away. Good vibes guaranteed.

WORM

Boomgaardsstraat 71, 3012 XA Cool (Centrum), worm.org

Add club WORM to your list when you feel like filling your Saturday night with DJ sets, live performances, or cultural activities. Lovers of techno, industrial, and experimental music will be right at home. Look at their calender for their ever-changing programme.

NOW & WOW

Maashaven Zuidzijde 1, 3081 AE Afrikaanderwijk (Feijenoord), insta @nowandwowclub

Dance like nobody's watching at NOW&WOW. Since they opened in 2000, they have organised countless electronic music events. Looking for a techno rave? Check NOW&WOW's Instagram page for their announcements.

THEATRES

Rotterdam will never be London, but you can still find some great theatres in the city. And the great thing is, there are plenty of shows for non-Dutchies too. Walhalla has performances that require no knowledge of Dutch at all – just check the calendar for 'Language no problem'. The same goes for Theater Rotterdam and De Doelen, who programme excellent shows and concerts. At both Luxor Theater and Oude Luxor, you can find English-spoken performances as well. And if you're up for a bit of fun, go to Club Haug for stand-up comedy in a lovely place near the Nieuwe Maas.

HOW TO DRESS LIKE A LOCAL

Modern and minimalistic with an urban twist. That's how we'd describe a trendy local's wardrobe. When you want to blend in, the first step – a very important one – is getting your hands on a SUSAN BIJL bag. The next step is finding the shops with (overpriced) sustainable brands, vintage, and second-hand items. Fast fashion is a big no go, although some well-known brands do have massive shops at Lijnbaan – once an iconic and luxurious shopping area in the city centre, now reduced to mainly fast fashion and fast food.

Casual streetwear is the way to go. So, leave your high heels at home. Swap them for cool trainers – the more exclusive, the better. Or some platform loafers, always with white socks pulled up high. Clothes-wise, it's all about the oversized look. Skinny jeans? Hell, no. Barrel jeans? Hell, yes! In winter, we keep it cool with big jumpers – baggy might as well be the local's middle name. Don't forget to wear a white tee underneath, at least if you want to be part of the 'cool' crowd. A puffer coat is a must when the weather is chilly. And a raincoat obviously belongs in every wardrobe. It might be in a standard colour, but a leopard print will also do the trick. Don't forget to bring your beanie, thick wool scarf and crossbody bag. During summertime, the fits are laid-back – just like the vibes in the city. In Rotterdam, it is all about timeless and functional fits instead of flashy trends. Once you remember to keep it cool and simple, you'll blend in easily.

SECOND-HAND & VINTAGE SHOPS

Think Twice

Karel Doormanstraat 355, 3012 GH Cool (Centrum), thinktwicevintage.nl

An empty closet but also an almost empty wallet? Head to Think Twice, one of the newest vintage (well, second-hand) shops in town. Colourful, sporty, or perfect for your next festival — they've got it. Keep an eye on their Instagram, as they often offer great discounts.

Cheap Fashion

Meent 25, 3011 JB Stadsdriehoek (Centrum), insta @ cheapfashionrotterdam

It's all in the name: the collection of Cheap Fashion is, yes, cheap. But it doesn't look it. Whether you're looking for summer dresses, checkered shirts, printed skirts or colourful trainers, the collection is full of fun items.

New X Archive

Pannekoekstraat 62A, 3011 LJ Stadsdriehoek (Centrum), newxarchive.com

High-end vibes all over. The prices at New X Archive are a bit higher, but the quality is pure gold. They offer a curated collection of new, deadstock, and pre-owned items. If you don't find anything here, you just need to look a bit harder. Just saying.

Old North Interiors

Burgemeester van Walsumweg 528, 3011 MZ Stadsdriehoek (Centrum), oldnorthinteriors.com

Whether you've just moved to Rotterdam and want to decorate your apartment with some authentic pieces or are just looking for inspiration: Old North Interiors is an interior design shop like no other. Their vintage, timeless pieces will bring a vibe to any lounge or bedroom.

SECOND-HAND & VINTAGE SHOPS

Rejoes

Oude Binnenweg 34 (1st floor), 3012 JE Cool (Centrum), rejoes.com

Do you easily get lost in thrift shops? Check out Rejoes's Instagram first (or the Lookbook on their website), get inspired, and then visit Oude Binnenweg. From sporty outfits to warm winter coats — and yes, they've got shoes too!

Dear Hunter Shop

Eendrachtsweg 55A, 3012 LE Cool (Centrum), insta @dearhunter.shop

Head straight to the Dear Hunter Shop if you want to spice up your wardrobe. This gem sells some fine vintage clothes and accessories. They don't keep items on hold or sell them online, so it's first come first served. Make sure you pop into the shop regularly.

Episode

Witte de Withstraat 19A, 3012 BL Cool (Centrum), episode.eu

Of course, one of the biggest European names in vintage also found its way to the streets of Rotterdam. And thank God. This branch of Episode has two floors that are filled with everything from warm jumpers to baggy jeans, and from sunnies to bags. Worth a trip.

Foreign Vintage

Oude Binnenweg 95A, 3012 JA Cool (Centrum), foreignvintage.nl

More is more — is that your mantra? Then don't skip a visit to Foreign Vintage. It doesn't matter if you're on the lookout for trainers, bomber jackets, jewellery or ripped jeans: they have it all. This shop is also a little paradise for everyone who loves designer items.

Marly Vintage

Schiedamse Vest 89B, 3012 BG Cool (Centrum), marlyvintage.com

We love a shop that mixes high-end designer items and more affordable pieces. Luckily, at Marly Vintage, they understand this desire, which results in a selection that warms the hearts of many fashion lovers. Fun fact: the shop is run by a fashionable father-daughter team.

Zwaanshals

Zwaanshals & Zaagmolenkade, Oude Noorden (Noord), zwaanshalskwartier.nl

Are you more into vintage than regular second-hand? Make sure you visit Zwaanshals. Along this street and Zaagmolenkade by the River Rotte, you'll find lots of great vintage shops. Ferme Tred focuses on designer items, Céno Classics and Hidden Youth stock a selection of great basics, and Komett Studios is also worth a visit. Make sure not to miss Showroom41 for some beautiful pieces.

Vintage aan de Rotte

Zwaanshals 468, 3035 KT Oude Noorden (Noord), vintagerotterdam.nl

Do you feel like bringing your Pinterest board to life? At Vintage aan de Rotte, you have a good chance of finding whatever you dream of. Their collection consists of all sorts of pieces from the 1960s and 1970s, from record players, vases and chairs to wine glasses and mirrors.

Studio Le Beau

Bergselaan 317A, 3038 CH Liskwartier (Noord), insta @studio_lebeau

Everything that Studio Le Beau offers – from chairs to paintings – will leave you feeling happy. The shop is full of items that warm artsy hearts. The fact that you can find winery Wijn bij Henk in the basement is just a fun extra. A win-win situation, if you ask us.

De Parel

Schiehaven 15B, 3024 EC Delfshaven-Schiemond (Delfshaven), insta @deparelrotterdam

Want to spice up your home or give your wardrobe a boost? At De Parel, they have a collection that always surprises. From chunky chairs and chests of drawers to fancy wine glasses and dresses. Visiting this gem isn't just fun, but timesaving as well: this is truly a one-stop shop.

Stil Leven Store

Nieuwe Binnenweg 316A, 3021 GV Middelland (Delfshaven), insta @stillevenstore

Beautiful items are found at the Stil Leven Store. Their curated, vintage design studio showcases high quality finds. Warning: there's a big chance that you'll leave with a bag or two in your hand. Their jaw-dropping collection makes it hard not to find the perfect fit.

VINTAGE MARKETS

Rotterdamse Oogst Markt

Noordplein 151, 3035 EC Oude Noorden (Noord), rotterdamseoogst.nl

At Rotterdamse Oogst Markt, some clothes will always pop up amongst the food stalls. Don't expect many vintage finds, though. What to expect? Some jewellery, accessories, and cool threads to add to your collection. It might be your lucky day.

Jouw Marktkraam

Zaagmolenkade 117, 3035 KD Oude Noorden (Noord), insta @jouwmarktkraam-rotterdam

When lovers of vintage, vinyl, bric-a-brac or homemade items bring their surplus to one spot, this will soon become a pretty cool spot. And that's what happened at Jouw Marktkraam. The shop has over twenty stalls where you can find nice and affordable gems. Or you could take part ...

OASE Vintage Markt

Schiehaven 15A, 3024 EC Delfshaven-Schiemond (Delfshaven), oaserotterdam.nl

The last Sunday of each month, Schiehaven turns into a vintage fashion and interior mecca. Make sure to get yourself a coffee before you start strolling past all the stands. A few are filled with cool jackets, while others sell badass jewellery or mirrors you just have to take home.

De Kaai Markt

Nassaukade 3, 3071 JL Katendrecht (Feijenoord), dekaaimarkt.nl

From blazers to hats your fashionable grandpa wore, and from leather bags to jewellery. Spice up your outfit at De Kaai Markt. The timing of the market varies, so make sure to check their website from time to time. You wouldn't want to miss it.

Waluw Vintage Market

insta @waluwvintagemarket

We have something cool in store for lovers of vintage fashion and interior design: we love Waluw Vintage Market. Every six months, the organisers surprise us with the coolest, local suppliers. Dates and locations are announced on their Insta.

STREETWEAR

Funkie House

Korte Hoogstraat 15A,
3011 GJ Stadsdriehoek
(Centrum), funkiehouse.nl

For over 35 years, Funkie House has kept the Rotterdam streetwear scene alive. Expect top-notch brands like Dickies and Patagonia, but also some cool items by Rotterdam locals. Their two-floor store makes it hard to leave empty-handed.

X21

Hoogstraat 169, 3011 PM
Stadsdriehoek (Centrum),
x21.nl

In an inconspicuous part of Hoogstraat, you will find this surprisingly hip shop for unique streetwear. They offer lesser-known brands and often have unique pieces in stock. X21 has done various collaborations on clothes, shoes, and accessories.

Carhartt WIP Store

Meent 24, 3011 JK
Stadsdriehoek (Centrum),
carhartt-wip.com

In Rotterdam, you won't just find the usual rack of Carhartt somewhere in a hidden corner, but a whole dedicated store with all your favourite streetwear. And the city centre location couldn't be better.

WOEI

Hoogstraat 44A, 3011 PS
Stadsdriehoek (Centrum),
woei-webshop.nl

Everyone who loves to treat their feet to some exclusive trainers head to WOEI. Some of their collaborations – with Stüssy, among others – make people queue for hours. Style them with their own brand of tees and crewnecks and you're good to go.

Skatestore

Westblaak 28, 3012 KM Cool (Centrum), skatestore.com

Next to skatepark Westblaak, you'll find the Skatestore. Besides apparel (naturally, you'd want to look good on your board), they have an enormous collection of skateboard decks, wheels, bearings, and trucks.

T0K10 Store

Van Oldenbarnevaltstraat 113-115, 3021 GS Cool (Centrum), tok10.com

High-end clothes and streetwear with a Japanese twist. That's what you'll find at T0K10. This shop is a true paradise for fashion lovers. Make sure to schedule some free time, as browsing the full collection might take a while.

Tom Coffee + Friends

Zaagmolenkade 41-42, 3035 KD Oude Noorden (Noord), insta @tom_coffeefriends

Sipping on an espresso while admiring local art and shopping for some new fits: at Tom Coffee + Friends, you can do it all. Tom himself will probably serve you. And his friends? They are the artists and brand owners he collaborates with.

↓ BLAUWCC, SEE PAGE 157

STREETWEAR

CONCEPT STORES

Anna + Nina

Pannekoekstraat 20a,
3011 JT Stadsdriehoek
(Centrum), anna-nina.nl

A brand best-known for their jewellery, such as the Never-Ending Bracelet that is welded on as it's fitted. They sell homeware and fashion too, their own designs as well as those by others. Most items have a fun twist, or to quote the founders of Anna + Nina: 'escape the ordinary'.

SUSAN BIJL

Nieuwe Binnenweg 94,
3015 BD Oude Westen
(Centrum)
insta @susanbijl

How to recognise a Rotterdam local? If they wear a colourful nylon SUSAN BIJL bag, chances are high. The bags are strong (amazing for your groceries), simple, and available in almost any colour combination. And you can get one too — we won't blame you. Also worth a visit: her backyard shop at Oostzeedijk 108 (Kralingen).

Zien & Corbeau

Nieuwe Binnenweg 60,
3015 BB Oude Westen
(Centrum), optiekzien.nl

Zien, 'see', is our favourite optician in town, with beautiful frames from Moscot among others, and cool sunglasses as well. Their eye tests are old-school thorough yet impressively modern. Corbeau, once located at Kruiskade as one of Rotterdam's oldest shoe shops, is now part of this store. The shoes made way for Peaky Blinders-style flat caps, silky leather gloves, and beautiful socks. You might want to bring the parents and their wallet if you want it all.

Marjolein Delhaas

Zaagmolenkade 170, 3035 KD Oude Noorden (Noord), shop.marjoleindelhaas.com

If you love structure, draw energy from finishing your to-do lists, or like to start your day journalling: Marjolein Delhaas has got you covered. Her minimalistic designs give your (home) office that extra productivity boost. Find just the right piece at her aesthetically pleasing shop.

BlauwCC

Zwaanshals 484, 3035 KS Oude Noorden (Noord), blauwcc.store

A gallery and concept store dedicated to beautiful things in blue! From postcards and clothing to little pieces of art, and larger items: blue, blue, blue. In any blue, from baby to navy. The shop's logo is in the famous hue by Yves Klein.

Rumours [concept] STORE

Lusthofstraat 57, 3061 WL Kralingen (Kralingen-Crooswijk), rumoursconceptstore.nl

Clothes, candles, jewellery, notebooks, little bags, big scarves, and the occasional art exhibition: Rumours [concept] STORE has it all. And we just love their friendly staff! Though this also might be one to bring the parents to.

↓ MARJOLEIN DELHAAS

BOOKSHOPS

Yendor

Korte Hoogstraat 16, 3011 GL Stadsdriehoek (Centrum), yendor.nl

Looking for a specific comic book, manga or graphic novel? At Yendor, they have been fulfilling fans' wishes since 1977. Just step inside the oldest comic shop in Rotterdam and have a browse.

De Kleine Kapitein

Botersloot 173, 3011 HE Stadsdriehoek (Centrum), de-kleine-kapitein.nl

A children's bookshop with a great YA department and a selection of board games that is worth the trip. And when you can't find anything for yourself – which we find hard to imagine – you can always treat your niece or nephew to a new book.

Donner

Coolsingel 129, 3012 AG Cool (Centrum), donner.nl

Looking for a specific title? At Donner, they probably have it – regardless of its genre. Entering this shop might feel a bit overwhelming, as they truly have everything. From books (obviously) and gifts to games. The English department is on the ground floor, YA can be found next to the travel guides, and there is a little café on the 2nd floor.

vanGennep

Oude Binnenweg 131B, 3012 JD Cool (Centrum), insta @boekhandelvangennep

A traditional literary bookshop, vanGennep has been around for about half a century. All this time, they have been providing Rotterdam with interesting books, from literature and poetry to art and photography books. If you don't already have a love for reading, the staff's enthusiasm is infectious.

PrintRoom

Schietbaanstraat 17, 3014 ZV Oude Westen (Centrum), printroom.org

Riso printing, or 'digital screen printing', is a lovely way to produce not just prints but zines and books as well. In addition to these printed objects, they also offer workshops and a range of events. We love their focus on international creatives, whose work you can find at PrintRoom.

NAi Bookstore

Museumpark 25, 3015 CB Dijkzigt (Centrum), naibooksellers.nl

Does architecture make your heart skip a beat? Always looking out for creative designs? Then head out to NAi Bookstore. It's the right spot to get your creativity flowing and expand your book collection. Also fun: the store is nestled at Nieuwe Instituut (see page 57).

KIOSK

Pieter de Raadtstraat 35, 3033 VC Provenierswijk (Centrum), kioskrotterdam.com

Yes, we do love paper — which is why we make books. And we do love little shops like this. At KIOSK, they are all about books, prints, zines, and more. They also organise writing groups and collaborative printing workshops.

Emma's Bookshop

Zwaanshals 432, 3035 KT Oude Noorden (Noord), emmasbookshop.nl

Do you romanticise bookshops a little? Well, at Emma's Bookshop this romance becomes reality. You may know Emma from her popular socials. If not, you won't forget her after visiting her shop. Expect to find (English) young adult books and some stationery designed by Emma herself.

Ver van Hier

Kleiweg 69, 3051 GJ Kleiwegkwartier (Hillegersberg-Schiebroek), insta @vervanhier

For a mix of coffee, books and cosy vibes, you should visit Ver van Hier. This is also a sure hit for finding gifts. If you have a young child in tow, they'll be occupied in the play area while you browse in peace.

Oosterboekhandel J.Amesz

Voorschoterlaan 145, 3062 KM Kralingen (Kralingen-Crooswijk), amesz-boekhandel.nl

When there's a book written about a bookshop, you know it must be special. At 125 years, Oosterboekhandel J.Amesz is Rotterdam's oldest bookshop. Tip: the friendly staff share their recommendations online. Most impressive of all is how up-to-date their stock is, despite the shop's modest size.

Bosch&deJong

Nico Koomanskade 1025, 3072 LM Katendrecht (Feijenoord), insta @boschendejong

Bosch&deJong is probably the smallest bookshop in town. A shop within a shop, it is part of the Fenix Food Factory. Browse the long wall of bookcases stocked with everything ranging from travel guides to literary fiction.

Boekhandel Maximus

Bergse Dorpstraat 122, 3054 GG Hillegersberg (Hillegersberg-Schiebroek)

Friendly neighbourhood bookshop Maximus offers a broad selection of titles. It is filled to the brim with novels, cookbooks, children's books, and of course travel guides.

BOOKSHOPS

GET CREATIVE

Meijer & Blessing

Westewagenstraat 27,
3011 AR Stadsdriehoek
(Centrum),
meijerenblessing.nl

Are you a fan of model construction? At Meijer & Blessing, they offer everything to do with model building; from train sets and model kits to glue, paint and tools, and even racetracks and steam engines. Their Star Wars collection is extensive. Anyone who loves building should plan a visit.

Gerstaecker

Hoogstraat 72, 3011 PT
Stadsdriehoek (Centrum)
gerstaecker.nl

Treat your inner artist to a new canvas, a paint palette, and some brushes. You might have hidden creative talents — a visit to Gerstaecker will reveal them. This is also a great place for pottery and craft supplies.

Van Beek Art Supplies

Hoogstraat 58-64, 3011 PT
Stadsdriehoek (Centrum),
vanbeekart.nl

A rainy Sunday is best filled with a creative session. If you feel like letting your creativity flow or want to learn how to draw, it's all possible at Van Beek Art Supplies. So, when do we meet up?

Schröder Modestoffen

Westblaak 61, 3012 KD
Cool (Centrum),
schrodermodestoffen.nl

Sewing and knitting enthusiasts should run to Schröder Modestoffen, which offers everything from fabrics to haberdashery. The only thing you need to find your inner fashion designer is to choose if you want to create your own linen trousers, corduroy jacket, or posh dress.

Hummelman

Stadhoudersweg 93A, 3039
EC Blijdorp (Noord), insta
@hummelmanpenshop

Joy can be found in the smallest things. The stunning fountain pens at Hummelman are proof. From classic to funky, writing will never be the same again. Their pens also make great gifts, especially paired with one of their notebooks.

SPICE UP YOUR HOME

HAY

Haagseveer 99, 3011 AH Stadsdriehoek (Centrum), hayinrotterdam.com

Does the minimalist in you crave new homeware? Then hurry to HAY, as this dreamy Scandi brand has a Rotterdam shop. Their furniture and accessories bring a trendy yet simple vibe to your home.

It's a Present

Witte de Withstraat 5, 3012 BK Cool (Centrum), itsapresent.nl

Everyone who's terrible at finding cool gifts should plan a visit to this shop. At It's a Present, they promise that they have a gift for literally everyone. Just imagine the time it would save if you'd go there and get it all sorted in one go.

Blend artwork + coffee

Nieuwe binnenweg 305A, 3012 GH Middelland (Delfshaven), insta @ blendartwork

It won't come as a surprise that Blend artwork + coffee is all about artwork and coffee. The place feels cosy and warm from the moment you walk in. Keep an eye out for their socials for updates on creative events such as drink & draw.

STEK de Stadstuinwinkel

Nieuwe Binnenweg 195B, 3021 GA Middelland (Delfshaven), insta @ stekdestadstuinwinkel

Decorating your balcony, adding some green to the living room or finding a gift: at STEK de Stadstuinwinkel you're sure to find a beautiful new plant for your garden, balcony or living room, or anything else to do with greenery. Check their secret garden for natural vibes in the middle of the city.

↓ STEK DE STADSTUINWINKEL

Het Derde Servies & Kleuroptafel

Nieuwe Binnenweg 208A, 3021 GL Middelland (Delfshaven), hetderdeservies.nl, kleuroptafel.nl

Tableware galore at these two shops sharing one address. It is the go-to spot for colorful plates, cups, linens, and more. A mix of antique, vintage, and new pieces, featuring brands from across Europe. A must-visit whether you're moving into a new home or keen on refreshing your cupboards.

Studio Soleil

Zwaanshals 410, 3035 KT Oude Noorden (Noord), studiosoleil.nl

Browns, beiges, and creams. From edgy chairs and aesthetic coffee table books to artistic paintings and plates to spice up the dinner table. You name it and Studio Soleil has it — all in neutral tones.

SPICE UP YOUR HOME

VINYL & CDs

Plato

*Nieuwe Binnenweg 13b,
3014 GA Oude Westen
(Centrum), platomania.nl*

In this part of town, vinyl lovers are already spoiled for choice, but Plato has to be on your radar too. They have an excellent selection of new records, especially hip-hop, and their vintage collection is slowly expanding. Check the website for live performances.

Velvet Music

*Oude Binnenweg 121A,
3012 JC Cool (Centrum),
insta @velvetrotterdam*

Discover your taste in music at this shop. The collection at Velvet Music includes everything from vinyl and CDs to DVDs. Make your visit even more fun by picking something random – it might become your go-to listen.

Plaatboef

*Nieuwe Binnenweg 81A,
3014 GE Oude Westen
(Centrum),
insta @plaatboefrotterdam*

A table filled with food, some red wine, and a vinyl collection on the side. At Plaatboef, you'll shop for second-hand vinyl and CDs to take home for a night in. Since 1981, locals have relied on them for a good selection of music.

Clone

*Raampoortstraat 12, 3032
AH Agniesebuurt (Noord),
clone.nl*

When a record label turns into a record shop, you know the owners are big music lovers. Although the label produced dance and house, you'll find any genre in the shop: from disco and jazz to funk and the obscure.

JensDo Records

*Zwaanshals 294B, 3035
KN Oude Noorden (Noord),
jensdorecords.nl*

We love one-stop shops. At JensDo Records, our wish was their command. Besides vinyl, they sell record players. Owner Jens is a music lover to the core and is always on the hunt for new records.

PARKS AND SWIMMING

Little C

Some compare the vibe and architecture at and views from Little C to New York City. And to be honest: we agree. In front of the building – which is filled with lunch spots and wine bars – you have a little piece of grassland where you can relax and take a refreshing dip in the water.

G.J. de Jonghweg, 3015 GE Dijkzigt (Centrum)

Euromastpark

The Euromast (see page 52) is blessed with some stunning views, with lunch spots like Parqiet and Dudok at its foot, as well as peaceful places to unwind. In summer, Euromastpark is where people bring their picnics while in winter, it's a lovely spot to go for a stroll.

Baden Powellaan 2, 3016 GJ Scheepvaartkwartier (Centrum)

Heemraadssingel

Many locals say that Heemraadssingel is the most beautiful canal in the city. The wooden bridges, imposing trees, and beautiful mansions create a romantic atmosphere, especially during spring. It connects Euromastpark to Vroesenpark.

Heemraadssingel, 3021 DA Middelland (Delfshaven)

Dakpark

A park on a roof, you'll find Dakpark nine metres above ground. This pocket of green is 1,200 metres long and 85 meters wide, claiming a spot on the list of 'Biggest rooftop parks of Europe'. As well as enjoying nature, you can play sports at Dakpark and relax.

Hudsonstraat 111, 3025 CE Bospolder-Tussendijken (Delfshaven)

Luchtpark Hofbogen

Yes, Rotterdam has a 1.9-kilometer-long park on a roof. And with that, it's the longest roof in the Netherlands. Quite something, isn't it? So, make your way up and enjoy a sunny lunch or walk along the allotments with a view of the skyline. You won't regret it.

Raampoortstraat 10, 3032 AH Agniesebuurt (Noord)

Vroesenpark

Opposite Blijdorp zoo, you'll find Vroesenpark. In winter, the grassy area is mainly used as a dog-walking spot, but during summer, it's a popular spot for groups of friends, families and solo sunbathers. Don't be surprised when you smell smoke: lighting the barbecue is popular here.

Stadhoudersweg 181, 3039 MC Blijdorp (Noord)

Roel Langerakpark

This park is a little different from others. All year round, it's a popular spot for music festivals. Not much of a dancer? It is also known for its sports facilities: it has an athletics track and a disc golf course. You'll also find an animal shelter and public garden in this park.

Roel Langerakweg 25, 3041 JK Blijdorp (Noord)

Het Kralingse Bos

Do you feel like escaping the buzz of the city? Head east. Het Kralingse Bos is, with its 250 hectares, Rotterdam's biggest park. You'll see sunbathers, runners, skaters, and even some sailboats. A visit to the petting zoo, having a go on the zip line, and spending a couple of hours at the climbing forest are other options.

Prinses Beatrixlaan 24, 3062 CM Crooswijk (Kralingen-Crooswijk)

Rotte

Curious where Rotterdam got its name? From the River Rotte. Back in the day, this river ran through the current city centre. Nowadays,

↓ KRALINGSE PLAS, THE LAKE IN HET KRALINGSE BOS

it goes under but comes above ground again near Noordplein. From there, we recommend renting a bike, picking a peaceful spot and taking a dip in the water.

Bergse Linker Rottekade, 3069 LV Molenlaankwartier (Hillegersberg-Schiebroek)

Rijnhaven

Swimming with a view of the Rotterdam skyline never loses its appeal. At the floating park on Antoine Platekade, a section has been designated for swimming. Spots like these make us wish that summer could last forever.

Antoine Platekade 995, 3072 ME Kop van Zuid (Feijenoord)

Eiland van Brienenoord

It may sound like an urban myth, but underneath the busy A16 motorway, you'll find a green island. Eiland van Brienenoord is located in the middle of the River Nieuwe Maas and is an officially designated swimming spot. You'll find it at the former construction dock (near the footbridge over Zuiddiepje, on the west side).

Van Brienenoord 5, 3077 AE Oud-IJsselmonde (IJsselmonde)

VEGETARIAN AND VEGAN ROTTERDAM

Backyard

Feel like kicking off the day with a strong cup of coffee? Go to Backyard! The same applies when you need some fuel for your day or want to end the evening with a festive drink. This plant-based restaurant is based in the city centre, and we couldn't be happier.

Korte Hoogstraat 14, 3011 GL Stadsdriehoek (Centrum), backyardrotterdam.nl

Copper Branch

Some places make the world a whole lot better, as they nourish our body and soul. Copper Branch is one of them. And a pretty good one; this plant-based restaurant was awarded Best Restaurant at the Dutch Horeca Awards in 2024. Good to know: their menu is also gluten-free.

Korte Hoogstraat 6, 3011 GL Stadsdriehoek (Centrum), insta @copperbranch_nl

Restaurant Rotonde

Restaurant Rotonde is one of the best places in Rotterdam for a laid-back, eco-conscious dinner. Not only does Rotonde's progressive kitchen take responsibility for Mother Earth, but the restaurant interior is also filled with recycled and vintage pieces. Bring the parents, just in case.

Goudsesingel 230, 3011 KE Stadsdriehoek (Centrum), restaurantrotonde.nl

Vegan Pizza Bar

Across the street from restaurant Rotonde, you'll find a vegan pizza bar. The tomato sauce on their pizza bases is topped with homemade vegan cheeses. Their menu ranges from a classic Margherita 2.0 to a funky Savage Sausage or a Korean-style K-pizza.

Goudsesingel 73, 3031 EE Stadsdriehoek (Centrum), veganpizzabar.com

Nori

Whenever you crave some Asian flavours, you know what to do. At least, now you do. The in-crowd goes to Nori for vegan sushi rolls worthy of a chef's kiss. Their stir-fried dishes and poké bowls are also popular. And all of these are vegan, too.

Pannekoekstraat 45A, 3011 LC Stadsdriehoek (Centrum), norirotterdam.nl

Crave Coffee & Bakery

If you're planning on eating healthier, you might want to skip this one. But if you're ready to give in to your cravings, you'll find it hard to choose between their pistachio croissants, lemon poppy cake, and oreo cake … At Crave Coffee Bakery, they make your sweet dreams come true.

Vogelenzang 6, 3011 LN Stadsdriehoek (Centrum), insta @cravecoffeebakery

Spirit & de Groene passage

Not so keen on fixed menus and limited options? At Spirit you can pick anything from their buffet that seems tasty – and there are about fifty different dishes to choose from. Located in de Groene Passage, the centre for conscious shoppers.

Mariniersweg 9, 3011 NB Stadsdriehoek (Centrum), spiritrestaurants.nl

Rozey

Rozey has an all-you-can-eat vegetarian and vegan menu. On weekends, you pay around 40 euros for food and drinks. The menu varies from crispy sushi rolls to quesadillas; there's something for everyone.

Wijnhaven 85, 3011 WK Stadsdriehoek (Centrum), rozey.nl

SUE

Sugar-free, gluten-free, and vegan: at SUE everyone can eat whatever they desire. The fact that the majority of the menu is pretty healthy doesn't mean that you won't find any sweet treats: their carrot cake and chocolate bars might be the main reason people go.

Karel Doormanstraat 372, 3012 GA Cool (Centrum); Goudsesingel 330, 3011 JT Cool (Centrum), insta @suefoodrotterdam

De Falafel

De Falafel isn't the prettiest of eateries, but the quality of their food — at low prices — is what brought them to this list. Their main ingredient — the falafel — is always made fresh, and at the salad bar you can make your order exactly what you want it to be. Perfect for a quick grab-and-go.

Binnenwegplein 11, 3012 KA Cool (Centrum)

Kula

Unwind while doing breathing exercises during a yoga class or savour a dish from their almost fully plant-based menu. At Kula you can do both. Preferably with a matcha latte on the side. Their *buffalo cauli wings* and *sticky tempeh bowl* are the bomb.

Abraham Tuschinskistraat 54, 3015 GK Dijkzigt (Centrum), kula.nl

Mecca Oasis

Rest. Recover. Connect. That's what Mecca Oasis is about. And their Middle Eastern dishes made from scratch. Did someone say *labneh*, *fattoush* or tahini brownie? Let's make that a double portion!

Noordsingel 39, 3035 EJ Agniesebuurt (Noord), meccaoasis.nl

Sajoer

A healthy juice a day keeps the doctor away. At Sajoer, you can pick up your juices for a one- to seven-day detox. Their smoothie bowls are very tasty, and their falafel wraps are always winning. Once a month, they transform their juice bar into a *toko*. What to expect? Well, tables filled with mouthwatering Indonesian meals, like *tempé*, *balado aubergine*, *sajoer beans*, *sambal goreng kentang*, and more.

Statenweg 141D, 3039 HL Blijdorp (Noord), sajoer.nl

VEGGIE

A vegan lunchroom, what's not to like? The owner of VEGGIE has Brazilian roots, which you will experience in everything she puts on your table. Besides the chai lattes, sandwiches and cakes – lots of cakes – their living-room vibes are a big reason for a visit.

Frits Ruysstraat 16A, 3061 ME Kralingen (Kralingen-Crooswijk), insta @veggie_rotterdam

De Oude Plek

De Oude Plek, 'the old place', is the one and only vegetarian (and even vegan) Chinese restaurant in town. No Peking Duck? That's right. But they do have Peking Seitan. Instead of meat, fish, or poultry, you can munch on loads of tasty veggies. De Oude Plek has been around for almost 25 years.

Pliniusstraat 18, 3076 AH IJsselmonde (South, near Feijenoord), deoudeplek.nl

OUTSIDE OF ROTTERDAM

Ackerdijkse Plassen

natuurmonumenten.nl

Between Rotterdam and Delft, you'll find the bird sanctuary Ackerdijkse Plassen. Enjoy a lovely walk with chirping birds and croaking frogs in the background. Don't forget to climb the observation tower, De Tureluur, for a view of the pond and the city's skyline. From Rotterdam Central Station, take the metro to Pijnacker (a 15-minute ride), and change to the bus to Oude Leedeweg (15 minutes).

Discover Rotterdam by water taxi

watertaxirotterdam.nl

If you have visited the city before, you probably spotted the little yellow boats on the River Maas. These water taxis have fifty different stops. From east and west to the city centre, and back. Travelling one stop costs 5 euros. Create your route online and explore Rotterdam from the water.

Delft

delft.nl

Dreamy canals, romantic courtyards, and buildings that take you back in time: strolling through Delft (a.k.a. 'Little Amsterdam') is something else. Do some sightseeing by visiting Oostpoort and Museum Prinsenhof. And don't forget to treat yourself to some delicious food at Il Tartufo or HANNO. From Rotterdam Central Station, there is a direct ten-minute train service to Delft.

Dordrecht & the city's green backyard

indordrecht.nl

While you can probably entertain yourself by hopping past all the bakeries (we love Hazel), boutiques and cosy canals in Dordrecht, you shouldn't forget the surrounding area. National Park De Biesbosch is breathtaking. Rent a bike and discover Dordrecht's green backyard. From Rotterdam Central Station, take the direct train service to Dordrecht (15 minutes).

Museum Voorlinden

voorlinden.nl

It is a little out of town, but once you arrive, you'll see a little piece of magic called Museum Voorlinden. It's not just the modern art museum that grabs your attention; its surroundings do a pretty good job too. The garden is stunning and connects nature to art. From Rotterdam Central Station, take a train to The Hague (30 min), and transfer on the bus to Wittenburgerweg (10 minutes).

↓ SCHIEDAM

↓ DELFT

Hoek van Holland Strand

Stationsweg 94, 3151 HS Hoek van Holland

Ready to breathe in some fresh air, have lunch with your feet in the sand, and enjoy a drink with sea views? In Hoek van Holland, you can do it all. After a long beach walk, we recommend you sit down and relax at Pele Surf Shack, De Pit or Uluwatu Beach. Chill vibes guaranteed. From Rotterdam Central Station, take the train to Schiedam Centrum (5 minutes), and transfer to the metro to Hoek van Holland Strand (30 minutes). Or take the direct metro from Beurs.

's-Gravenzande

Slag Vlugtenburg, 2691 KW 's-Gravenzande

Surfing in the Netherlands? From central Rotterdam, you'll reach the waves within thirty minutes by car or in an hour by metro. Tip: book a beginner or intermediate class at Dutch Surf Academy. From Rotterdam Central Station, take the train to Schiedam Centrum (5 minutes), and transfer to the metro to Hoek van Holland Strand (30 minutes).

IJsselmonde

ontdekijsselmonde.nl

Between Oude Maas and River Noord, you'll find beautiful nature reserves that are part of the island of IJsselmonde. This peaceful area has lots of walking and cycling trails. Online, you can find the one that suits you best. Whichever you choose, make sure to keep an eye out for any wildlife roaming around. From Rotterdam Central Station, take the tram to Adriaan Volkerlaan (30 minutes).

UNESCO World Heritage Kinderdijk

kinderdijk.nl

Hop on the Waterbus or take the train to Kinderdijk – a UNESCO World Heritage Site since 1997. The entire area lies below sea level, which has kept the residents working to keep their feet dry for centuries. Delve into its history and explore the windmills to fully experience it. From Rotterdam Central Station, take the train to Dordrecht (15 minutes), and transfer to the bus to Molenkade (40 minutes).

Schiedam

sdam.nl

The old city of Schiedam has plenty to offer. From stand-up paddleboarding through the canals to renting a small boat with your friends. When it's time to get back onto land, have a matcha topped with pistachios at Café Schattig or order small bites to share at restaurant 1714. From Rotterdam Central Station, take the direct service to Schiedam Centrum (5 minutes).

↓ 'S GRAVENZANDE

↓ ACKERDIJKSE PLASSEN

INDEX

Neighbourhoods 8
Practical info 12
Travel 14
Where to stay 18
Good to know 22
When to travel 28
History 40
Street art 64
Cinema 70
Festivals 72
Things to do 76
Famous people 78
Films & series in and about Rotterdam 84
Books in & about Rotterdam 88
Fun facts 94
Food and drinks 104
Going out 128
Green Rotterdam 168
Parks and swimming 172
Vegetarian and vegan Rotterdam 177
Outside of Rotterdam 182

SIGHTSEEING 48

Delfshaven 53
Erasmusbrug 48
Euromast 52
Floating Farm 53
Kubuswoningen 52
Laurenskerk 48
Markthal 49
Oude Haven 49
ss Rotterdam 54
Van Nellefabriek 54
Veerhaven 52

MUSEUMS & GALLERIES 56

Brutus 61
Chabot Museum 58
Depot Boijmans van Beuningen 58
Fenix 60
Galerie Vivid 56
Galerie Wind 59
Huidenclub 61
Huis Sonneveld 58
Kunstcblock 56
Kunsthal 56
Museum Rotterdam '40-'45 NU 59
Natuurhistorisch Museum 57
Nederlands Fotomuseum 60
Nieuwe Instituut 57
Wereldmuseum 59

PHOTO SPOTS 98

Depot Boijmans van Beuningen 101
Erasmusbrug 98
Fenix 103
Hotel New York 102
Kralingse Plas 102
Kubuswoningen 98
Little C 101
Markthal 98
Skyline 102
Wilhelminapier 101

FOOD AND DRINKS 104

21 pinchos Fenix 125
Arzu 107
Bakeries 110
Bakkit 113
Ballentent, De 123
Bar Bù 127
Bar Dertien 125
Bar Pulpo 123
Bazaar 119
Bonte Keukentafel, De 114
Bonza Koffie 110
Bram Ladage 116
Breakfast 106
By Jarmusch 106
Bring the parents 127

Brunch & lunch 113
Bun 114
Burgertrut 121
Coppi 110
Dinner 117
Drippy's Burgers 116
Dudok 110
Fries & snacks 116
Frietboutique 116
Guliano 113
Harvest Café & Bakery 112
Hotel New York 125
Hung Kee 119
Jordy's Bakery Rotterdam 112
Kiem Foei 121
Kiiro 117
Klaargemaakt 124
Koekela 112
Little Italy 113
Little V 117
Louise Petit Déjeuner 106
Maaskantine 117
Machinist aan de Cool, De 124
Man met Bril Koffie 106
Marseille, Café 122
Masa 123
Matroos en het meisje 126
NICE 107
Nine Bar 107
On Other Drugs 114
Parqiet 106
Paviljoen aan het water 126
Petit Jean, Le 112
Pomms 116
RDM Kantine 116
Rijntje 127
Rottiedam 125
Silbar 124
Social 107
Soi3 122
Souq, Le 123
Sranang 121
Station Bergweg 124
Station Café 114
Supermercado 119
Tai Wu 121
THE GOAT 117
Tres 127
Urban Espresso Bar 110
Vislocale Kaap 127
Warung Mini 119
Wolly 113
Yokohama Ramen Salto 126

GOING OUT 128
160K 138
Amehoela 131
Annabel 137
Bakkeliet 136
Beer 133
Bierboutique 134
Biergarten 134
BIRD 138
Bokaal 133
Botanero 130
Café de Schouw 133
Café de Witte Aap 134
Café Steijn 136
Café Verward 130
Club Haug
Clubs 137
Doelen, De 139
Ferry's 137
Juni 133
Kaapse Maria 134
Keerweer 136
Keilecafé 136
Luxor + Oude Luxor 139
MONO 138
Nord, Le 132
NOW & WOW 139
OX Rotterdam 131
Perron 137
Proeflokaal Reijngoud 133
Queer 136
Rotown 137
Rumah, The 130
Soirée, La 131
Spikizi 131
Theater Rotterdam 139

189

Theatres 139
Toffler 138
Walhalla 139
Walsjerot 132
Wijnbar het Eigendom 130
Wine & cocktails 130
WORM 139

SHOPPING 140
How to dress like a local 142

Bookshops 158
Boekhandel Maximus 160
Bosch&deJong 160
Donner 158
Emma's Bookshop 160
KIOSK 159
Kleine Kapitein, De 158
Nai Bookstore 159
Oosterboekhandel J. Amesz 160
PrintRoom 159
vanGennep 159
Ver van Hier 160
Yendor 158

Concept stores 156
Anna + Nina 156
BlauwCC 157
Marjolein Delhaas 157
Rumours [CONCEPT] Store 157
SUSAN BIJL 156
Zien & Corbeau 156

Get creative 162

Second-hand & vintage shops 144
Cheap Fashion 144
Dear Hunter Shop 146
Episode 146
Foreign Vintage 146
Jouw Marktkraam 148
Kaai Markt, De 149
Marly Vintage 147
New X Archice 144
OASE Vintage Markt 149
Old North Interiors 144
Parel, De 148
Rejoes 146
Rotterdamse Oogst Markt 148
Stil Leven Store 148
Studio Le Beau
Think Twice 144
Vintage aan de Rotte 147
Vintage markets 148
Waluw Vintage Markt 149
Zwaahals 147

Spice up your home 164

Streetwear 152
Carhartt WIP Store 152
Funkie House 152
Skatestore 153
TOK10 Store 153
Tom Coffee + Friends
WOEI 152
X21 152

Vegetarian & vegan Rotterdam 177
Backyard 177
Copper Branch 177
Crave Coffee & Bakery 178
Falafel, De 179
Kula 179
Mecca Oasis 180
Nori 178
Oude Plek, De 180
Restaurant Rotonde 177
Rozey 179
Sajoer 180
Spirit & de Groene passage 178
SUE 179
Vegan Pizza Bar 177
VEGGIE 180

Vinyl & CD's 166

ABOUT THE AUTHORS

Lotte van Zijl

Dreamer, fashion-lover, and wannabe surf girl Lotte is a Rotterdam-based freelance journalist. Besides writing, she loves to travel — preferably to sunny spots known for their cuisine — dance to soul, house, or R&B tunes, and get her hands on vintage finds. She grew up near Rotterdam, and no matter how busy she is travelling the world, this creative city will always have her heart. Find her shopping for vintage on Zwaanshals, sipping wine at Le Nord or dancing the night away at Biergarten.

Sylvia Meijer-Villafane

Sylvia came to Rotterdam for love and never left. She has lived in Rotterdam West for many years but feels at home in the entire city. Her favourite pastime? Recommending restaurants to friends and family — whether they ask for it or not. But only after she's tried them herself, of course. She also loves hunting for vintage gems in and around Zwaanshals, having wine and *bitterballen* at her favourite bar Café Steijn, or taking a stroll around Kralingse Plas.

WHY SHOULD I GO TO ROTTERDAM
the city you definitely need to visit
before you turn 30 (or 130)

Published in 2025 by
mo'media Rotterdam,
The Netherlands, momedia.nl

Concept
mo'media

Text and address selection
Sylvia Meijer-Villafane, Lotte van Zijl

Art direction and illustration design
Jelle F. Post

Editing
Maaike van Steekelenburg, Ezra van Wilgenburg

Photography
Vincent van den Hoogen,
Petra de Hamer, Sylvia Meijer-Villafane

All rights reserved. No part of this publication may be copied, displayed, extracted, reproduced, utilised, stored in a retrieval system or transmitted in any form or by any means, electronic, mechanical or otherwise including but not limited to photocopying, recording, or scanning without the prior written permission of the publisher.

(m) Copyright © mo'media BV, 2025

Why Should I Go To Rotterdam
ISBN 978 94 9333 870 8
NUR 510

Disclaimer
The points of interested mentioned in this travel guide have been selected by the author. None of them have been paid for inclusion in this book: the *Why Should I Go To* book series is entirely ad-free.

Publisher's Note
Every effort has been made to ensure that the information in this book is accurate at the time of going to press. The publisher welcomes any information or suggestions for correction or improvement. Please send us an e-mail at info@momedia.nl.

 whyshouldigoto

WHY SHOULD I GO TO?
Information on all our travel guides
on **WHYSHOULDIGOTO.COM**

Why Should I Go To travel guides are available for the following cities: Amsterdam, Antwerp, Barcelona, Berlin, Budapest, Copenhagen, London, Paris, Prague, Rome and Valencia. More cities will be added soon.